Golf

The Fundamentals

Golf
The Fundamentals

THIRD EDITION

Frank Ormond
Charles E. Patch

CAROLINA ACADEMIC PRESS
Durham, North Carolina

ISBN 0-89089-344-6
LCCN 2003109201

Carolina Academic Press
700 Kent Street
Durham, NC 27701
Telephone (919) 489-7486
Fax (919) 493-5668
www.cap-press.com

Printed in the United States of America

Contents

Preface

Golfers come from all walks of life, and while some start at an early age, an increasing number of others come to golf much later in their lives. The reasons for starting the game may vary widely, but there is a uniqueness to the game of golf that keeps millions of players coming back again and again. The significance of the competitive aspects of the game of golf is appealing to many players. In addition, there is a profound personal enjoyment to be found in being out of doors in the natural environment on the golf course; there is an opportunity to be with friends or to meet new ones; there is the potential to improve individual fitness and to reduce stress; and finally, there is the ultimate individual challenge to be found in attempting to improve your golf game. This book has been written to assist the early golfer, the beginner, as well as the more advanced players seeking to improve their skills. Fundamentals are stressed for all golfers, including how to hold the club correctly and how to assume a natural and athletic posture. Checkpoints within the swing are introduced and should be used as guides in developing the best swing for you. Players at all skill levels will find information on how to correct some of golf's most frequent swing errors, with accompanying practice drills to assist in developing a more repeatable and consistent swing. In addition to sections specifically dealing with the golf swing, chapters have also been included to address the history of golf, the rules and etiquette of the game, up-to-date information relating to equipment, and finally, some thoughts and ideas relating to golf course management. It is our hope that this text will improve your understanding of the various aspects of the game of golf, thus enabling you—with equal measures of practice and play—to both improve your skill level and your enjoyment of the game. The game of golf has been described as a "journey"—we hope that yours is an exciting one!

Acknowledgments

The authors wish to thank the following individuals for their contributions to this book:

Linda Lacy for her editorial assistance.

Joel V. Brothers for his efforts as "first reader."

Tim Colton for the book design and layout.

Todd Gilmore for the illustrations.

Doug Sheppard for the photographs.

Jessie Bunn, Tom Evans, Robert Hughes, and Henry Kidd for being models for photographs.

Carolina Custom Golf Co., Raleigh, N.C., Prestonwood Country Club, Cary, N.C., and Raleigh Golf Association, Raleigh, N.C. for allowing photographs to be taken at their facilities.

Mid Pines Inn & Golf Club, Southern Pines, N.C. for the beautiful cover photo of the 13th hole at Mid Pines. Mid Pines is a 1921 Donald Ross-designed golf course with 112 rooms in the Georgian-style Inn and villas situated on the 10th fairway. Its sister property, Pine Needles Lodge and Golf Club, was the host site of the 1996 and 2001 US Women's Open Championships and will host the Championship again in 2007. www.pineneedles-midpines.com 800-747-7272.

And finally, Robert G. Gwyn for his efforts in establishing this instructional textbook.

Golf
The Fundamentals

1 Golf: The Game for a Lifetime

The game of golf is much the same today as the game played in Europe over 500 years ago. After its introduction in the United States, organized golf grew at a steady pace until the 1960s when its popularity increased tremendously. Several factors, including popular players like Arnold Palmer, increased television coverage (golf is the only sport which has a television channel devoted to it 24 hours, 7 days a week), the electric golf cart, and a more affluent society with more leisure time, combined to produce this growth spurt. By the 21st century there were in excess of 25 million golfers in the United States alone, who spend over a billion dollars each year on golf equipment.

The Origins

While a game quite similar to golf as we know it today was being played in parts of Holland as early as the 13th century, it disappeared from records for unknown reasons. It is also believed that golf may have been played in Scotland as early as the 13th century. However, the first documented evidence of the game in that country did not emerge until the mid-15th century, when King James II of Scotland banned the game so that his people would have more time to practice archery, a skill necessary for national defense. By the early 16th century the sport had rebounded and was being played in most parts of Scotland. King James I of England introduced the game to the English in the early part of the 17th century (Peper, 1999).

Golf grew in popularity and spread across the British Isles, however, it was not organized, except at the local level. In the mid-18th century the Honorable Company of Edinburgh Golfers began playing golf according to a written set of rules. These first 13 rules form the nucleus of the 34 rules used worldwide by golfers today. It was over 100 years after the original rules were written that open, championship golf was first played. In 1860, the British Open became the first official golf tournament. The British Open is still played today and is one of the four tour-

Fig. 1.1. Golf then. Left: Katharine Harley, 1908 U.S. women's champion. Right: Unidentified golfer, ca. 1910.

naments (British Open, United States Open, The Masters, and PGA) that make up the modern-day Grand Slam of golf. The British Amateur was first played in 1885, shortly after the St. Andrews Society of Golfers was reorganized to become the now famous Royal and Ancient (R&A) Golf Club of St. Andrews.

The earliest documentation that golf was being played in the United States comes from court records and business transactions. These reports show evidence that golf was equipment was being shipped to locations on the East Coast, most notably Charleston, South Carolina and Savannah, Georgia, in the mid-eighteenth century. However, the first recognized golf club was not organized until 1888, in Yonkers, New York (Henderson and Stirk, 1985). The first incorporated golf club in the United States was established four years later at Shinnecock Hills, NY. Shinnecock Hills was also the first club to build a clubhouse. Most recently, Shinnecock Hills played host to the U.S. Open in 1985, the Centennial U.S. Open in 1995, and will host the U.S. Open again in 2004.

Tournament play in the United States began in 1895 with the U.S. Amateur, and the Men's and Women's Opens. These tournaments were organized by the United States Golf Association (USGA), which had been formed the previous year. Today, the USGA organizes and runs the top amateur tournaments in the United States. The Professional Golf Association (PGA) was formed in 1916 to certify and administer the professional golfers who serve at courses across the country providing expert instruction and promoting golf as a game for people of all ages and skills levels. The PGA also administers professional golf tournaments through the PGA Tour, which includes over 40 tournaments each year. The Ladies Professional Golf Association (LPGA), formed in 1950, is the oldest continuous women's sports association in the world. In 2003, the LPGA sponsored 34 events with an average purse of $1.2 million. The Champions Tour, formerly the Senior Tour, was formed in 1980 for professional golfers age 50 and older and offers golfers the opportunity to extend their careers much longer than athletes in other sports. The Champions Tour has over 30 tournaments offering almost $60 million in prize money in 2003. Because of escalating tournament purses, many of the players on the Champions Tour have earned more in five years than they did in an entire career on the PGA Tour. It also offers the hope or a dream for some who could not make it on the PGA Tour to play professional golf.

Fig. 1.2. Golf now.

The increasing popularity of golf extends worldwide. Through television coverage of international competitions such as the World Match Play Championship, the Ryder Cup, Walker Cup, Solheim Cup and the Curtis Cup, golf has become visible to people in countries where golf was not widely played. As a result, new courses open every day all over the world, and millions of people take up the game each year.

Benefits of Golf

Golf can be described as a game for all seasons and all reasons. Except for the northernmost parts of the U. S. where the winters restrict play, most players enjoy playing year-round. Year-round play affords golfers the opportunity to experience and appreciate the change in the seasons. As a lifetime activity, golf provides many benefits—physical, psychological, and social. "Not only do you use your muscles, you use your mind. A good round of golf leaves you pleasantly satisfied physically, mentally and emotionally" (Penick, 1992).

Unlike more physically demanding sports, golf does not require any special physical attributes such as being exceptionally tall, fast or strong. In fact, some of the most successful golfers on the professional tours are not exceptional in any of these characteristics. This is not to say, however, that a certain amount of flexibility and strength is not helpful. A more flexible person will be able to produce a longer swing arc, which will allow that person to generate more clubhead speed, thus more distance. A stronger person will be able to generate more clubhead speed without having to "over swing" the club.

The physical benefits of golf are more rewarding if you walk while you play rather than ride in a motorized golf cart. In a typical 18-hole round of golf you will walk an average of five miles. This walk helps increase your cardiorespiratory fitness and helps control your weight. Riding in a motorized golf cart negates most of these benefits. Carrying your clubs and walking provide the most physical benefits, using a pull cart or a caddy allows you to enjoy the benefits of the walk without the burden of carrying your golf bag. Motorized golf carts have no practical purpose for the younger and healthier golfer, they do provide people whose physical capabilities have been diminished due to age or physical limitations the opportunity to play the game. This has enabled thousands of people who would otherwise have been physically incapable of walking the whole course to continue to enjoy the game.

When approached with the attitude that it is a game, not a threat to your self-esteem, golf can provide the psychological benefits of relieving tension and stress by offering you the opportunity to relax and rejuvenate yourself. If you walk as you play, you are afforded the unique opportunity to enjoy the sport at your own pace while enjoying a beautiful day in the great outdoors. Worldwide, golf is played on some of nature's most stunning landscapes just waiting for you to delight in their beauty.

The social aspect of golf is another attraction of the game. A trip to the golf course provides the chance to meet many new friends or enjoy the company of old friends or family. Many find this opportunity to meet new people on a regular basis to be a rewarding experience. Others are content to play with the same group of friends each week. Still others like the idea of being able to spend time with their families, something that is often hard to do during a busy workweek.

The increasing popularity and growth golf has enjoyed, especially over the past 30 years, did not happen by accident. The physical benefits from walking, the relief of stress, the joy of making new friends or spending time with old friends and family, combine to make golf one of life's most rewarding experiences. The game of golf has often been de-

Fig. 1.3. Friendships made on the golf course are forever.

scribed as a journey. You will always be learning something new, yet never quite mastering the game. This journey can be long and rewarding, beginning in early childhood and continuing throughout your lifetime.

2 Equipment: Selection and Care

The object of golf, getting the ball from the tee into the hole in the least number of strokes, is the same for every golfer. However, the method of achieving this objective will vary depending on personal preferences and the particular set of circumstances involved in every shot. Because of all the factors that influence each shot, the equipment manufacturers have produced a variety of different types of clubs to facilitate this objective.

With a seemingly endless number of choices in clubs and other equipment the question becomes, "Where do you begin?" Do you purchase new or used clubs, steel or titanium woods, cast or forged irons, steel or graphite shafts, large or standard size grips, 2- or 3-piece golf balls, etc.? As a starting point, you should understand that under Rule 4-4, you are limited to a carrying maximum of 14 clubs. This does not necessarily mean, however, that you need to go out and purchase a full set of clubs. You might chose to buy a set of used clubs that consists of a 3-wood, a 5-wood, a few irons, and a putter. This would significantly

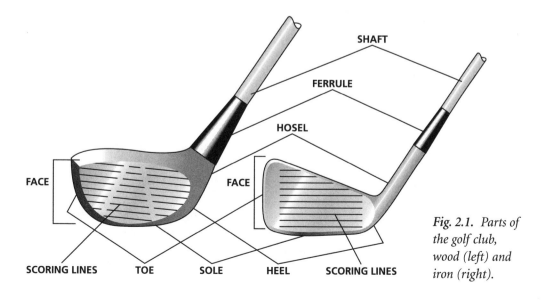

Fig. 2.1. Parts of the golf club, wood (left) and iron (right).

9

reduce the initial expense of equipment when you first take up the game. If you decide that you enjoy the game enough to play more frequently, and you begin to develop a better feel for your swing so that you are able to consistently make solid contact with the ball, then the price of a full set of new clubs might be justified. Making solid contact with the ball in the sweet spot of the clubface allows you to take advantage of the ability to get different distances and trajectories from the different clubs.

When you are ready to purchase a new set of clubs, the best place to start is with your local golf professional, or a golf specialty store. Your golf professional and golf specialist generally offer some advantages over local wholesale and discount department stores. A golf pro and specialist are well trained to assist you in purchasing a set of clubs that will fit your individual physique and swing. They also offer a higher quality product, which they will usually allow you to test before purchasing. In addition, they stand behind the equipment they sell by repairing or replacing it when necessary.

A set of clubs can be broken down into 3 categories: metal woods, irons, and putters. The woods are normally numbered 1 through 5, and are used mainly for tee shots and long fairway shots. The use of more lofted fairway woods has become popular in the last several years with more people purchasing a 7, 9 and even an 11-wood. Some manufacturers have also begun to replace the long irons with hybrid clubs, a cross between a fairway wood and a long iron (Figure 2.7). These clubs have more mass lower in the club making it easier to get the ball airborne than it is with a long iron. These hybrid clubs are very useful when hitting out of the light rough because they have enough loft to get the ball airborne out of the tall grass, and their wide sole and short hosel make the club less resistant to twisting in the tall grass.

The irons are numbered 1 through 9, and are used for approach shots of varying distances. They are also used for tee shots on par-3's, and on par-4 and par-5 holes where accuracy off the tee is more important than distance. There is no specific distance that you will hit with each of your irons. Instead, the distance that you get with each iron will vary depending on your skill level and physical attributes. The specialty irons that most golfers carry are the wedges (pitching, sand and lob wedges, Figure 6.1). The wedges are normally used for hitting short shots near the green and for shots such as hitting over a tree or a steep bank where the ball must get up quickly and fly on a high trajectory. The sand wedge has a sole that is specially designed to allow the clubhead to bounce out of the sand, making bunker shots much less difficult. The sand wedge can also be used from the fairway and for shots out of deep rough. The lob wedge is a more recent addition to the wedge family and usually has a 60° loft. The high loft of this club allows you to make a longer swing on shots that are close to the green. This is an advantage for golfers who have difficulty controlling the distance on shots that do not require a full swing. Shots with the lob wedge have a high trajectory and a high rate of spin causing the shot to land softer and stop quicker once it hits the green. The lob wedge can also be used for sand shots when the sand is wet or hard packed and for shots out of deep rough.

Choosing the Woods and Irons

Prior to purchasing a new set of clubs there are seven important variables about a club that you should be familiar with: clubhead design, shaft, length, lie, loft, swing weight and grip.

Clubhead Design

Woods

The designation "wood" may actually be slightly confusing to the novice due to the predominance of metal woods that has occurred since the early 1980s. Prior to the 1980s woods were actually made of wood, most commonly, persimmon or maple. With the introduction of metal woods (Figure 2.2), steel ("Pittsburgh Persimmon") quickly became the most popular choice in "wood" clubhead design, and for good reasons. Metal woods are cast in a mold, making them relatively inexpensive to mass-produce. As titanium and some of the new steel alloys were introduced, metal woods became much lighter. A lighter clubhead allows for greater clubhead speed, which produces more distance on the shot. As the alloys became lighter this also allowed the club manufacturers to make metal woods with larger clubheads. Some of the metal woods available on the market today are over 500cc in size.

As metal woods have become larger, the clubface has become thinner. The thinner clubface provides a trampoline or spring-like effect, producing a higher initial velocity and more distance on the shot. This

Fig. 2.2. Metal woods.

spring-like effect is measured as the Coefficient of Restitution (C.O.R). The USGA and the R&A have recently put a limit of .830 on the clubface C.O.R. Lighter weight also allows the weight to be redistributed in the clubhead to provide a larger sweet spot and a higher launch angle. A larger sweet spot makes the club more forgiving on mishits and a higher launch angle gets the ball airborne more easily resulting in more carry and more overall distance. I think you can see the theme behind metal woods. Their lighter weight, larger size and sweet spot and their higher C.O.R make metal woods more forgiving, more accurate and capable of more distance than the old wooden woods. The recent limits set by the USGA and the R&A on clubface C.O.R. and pending limits on the size of metal wood clubheads are necessary. Without these limits, clubhead and ball technology threaten to make many courses obsolete for professionals because they cannot be lengthened. On the other hand, this same technology has made the game easier and more enjoyable for the average player.

Irons

The clubhead design of irons falls into two major categories—forged and cast (Figure 2.3). Forged irons originate from a thick rod of steel. This rod of steel is stamped into the rough shape of the clubhead that then goes through several finishing steps prior to a chrome finish to produce the final product. Cast irons—which are made by pouring molten metal into a mold—require fewer steps, making them less expensive and faster to produce. The perimeter weighting of the cast club also produces a larger sweet spot and a lower center of gravity than that of a forged club. The larger sweet spot, as in metal woods, makes the club more forgiving on off-centered hits, resulting in a more consistent shot pattern. The lower center of gravity gives a higher launch angle, making it easier to get the ball airborne. While cast irons are a much better choice for the average golfer, many professionals and top amateurs prefer forged irons, claiming that they have a more traditional look and "softer" feel than cast clubs.

Technology has allowed club manufacturers to make the game easier and more enjoyable for the average golfer. While changes in clubhead ma-

Fig. 2.3. Forged (F) and cast (C) irons.

terials, size and design have received the most publicity, other factors have improved the playability of golf clubs. Club manufacturers have altered the standard length and loft of irons, and have made custom fitting of clubs a higher priority. Today, irons are, on average, ½ inch longer and have three to four degrees less loft than they did 25 years ago. This effectively makes the modern 5-iron the same length and loft of the older 4-iron. This change in length and loft is consistent throughout the set. The increased attention to custom fitting clubs has been of great benefit to the average golfer by making clubs more playable. Professionals have always had their clubs custom designed. The average golfer was forced to buy a standard set off the rack and fit his or her swing to the clubs rather than fitting the clubs to the swing. By taking advantage of improved club technology and having your clubs custom fitted, you will be able to improve your shot making and your enjoyment of the game.

Shafts

Of the seven factors that should be considered when choosing a set of clubs, the selection of the correct shaft is considered by many to be the most important. The shaft, then, is the engine that makes the rest of the club—and golfer—work. It is the one piece of equipment that can be changed and effect immediate results in your shots—without his changing anything else. When buying clubs from a wholesale or discount department store, you will be able to purchase less expensive sets of clubs, however, they usually have poorer quality shafts. Poor quality, unmatched shafts do not provide the same feel in each club, and they produce a much wider shot pattern. Your golf professional can custom fit the shaft for your swing.

You should start by determining the correct flex for your shafts. Swing speed, shaft loading, the average carry distance of your driver, and/or the distance that you hit your 7-iron are common measures used to determine which shaft flex is correct for you. Shafts that flex more easily provide more feel as the weight of the clubhead flexes the shaft, and they can add some distance to your shots. Stiffer shafts are more of an advantage when consistency and control of your shot patterns is of more concern than distance. Most professionals and top amateurs generate enough clubhead speed to produce sufficient distance; therefore, they will use a stiffer shaft to get tighter, more consistent, shot patterns. If the shaft in your clubs is too stiff, your shots will tend to fly to the right with a lower trajectory. If your shafts are too weak, your shots will fly higher than normal and to the left. The standard advice is to choose the lightest, most flexible shaft that you can control.

Shot trajectory is another aspect of the shot that is receiving attention from the shaft manufacturers. Today you can order shafts with different bend points. The lower the bend point, the higher the trajectory of the shot. This is beneficial to players who have a difficult time getting the ball airborne. Players who generate a lot of clubhead speed will usually opt for a shaft with a higher bend point to give their shots a lower trajectory and more distance.

Options are also available for fine-tuning shafts. They include choosing the weight of the shaft, frequency matching the shafts and "pureing" the shafts. Royal Precision shafts are frequency matched, meaning that the clubs have the same identical flex throughout the set. Golfsmith offers "SST PUREing" which is a computerized shaft analysis system that provides the correct shaft orientation to counter the inconsistencies within each shaft to give the most consistent oscillation patterns possible in a shaft. This type of attention to detail in shaft selection will optimize your clubs' performance, leaving nothing to chance.

Over the past century, club manufacturers have experimented with different shaft construction materials for shafts to replace wood. Some of these materials include steel, aluminum, fiberglass, titanium and graphite. Of these, steel, the material that first began to replace wooden shafts in the 1920s, has been the most popular. Most recently, graphite shafts have received more attention, as the manufacturing process has been refined, allowing for a more consistent product than early versions. Some professionals and many average golfers have begun to replace their steel shafts with the improved graphite shafts. This is because graphite shafts are lighter than steel.

With the introduction of lighter metal clubheads and lighter graphite shafts, woods are typically longer than the old standard of 43½ inches. Many golfers are playing with metal drivers that are close to 45 inches in length. The longer shaft produces more clubhead speed due to the longer swing arc, resulting in longer distances. Graphite shafts also absorb shock better than steel shafts, which helps reduce wear and tear on the joints of the hands, wrists and elbows. The biggest deterrent to graphite shafts, however, is their expense. Whether graphite shafts will succeed in overtaking steel as the material of choice for shafts will depend on the manufacturers' ability to reduce costs and further improve their consistency.

Length

The standard length of a driver is 43½ inches for men and 42½ inches for women. The standard 2-iron is 39½ inches for men and 38½ inches for women. Each subsequent wood or iron is ½ inch shorter than the driver or 2-iron (i.e., for men, a 2-wood = 43 inches, 3-wood = 42½ inches, a 3-iron = 39 inches, a 4-iron = 38½ inches, etc.). The standard length for clubs is about ½ inch longer than the standard 25 years ago. The standard-length clubs will fit the swing of most golfers. If you think you need clubs that are longer or shorter than standard, be sure to consult with a trained professional who can custom fit your clubs. A recent trend that runs counter to using standard length clubs concerns the length of the driver. Several manufacturers are beginning to produce drivers, particularly those with graphite shafts, that are 45 inches or more in length. The advantage is a longer swing arc, which creates more clubhead speed and thus longer tee shots—something that most golfers are constantly seeking. The disadvantage to consider with the longer driver is the possible loss of accuracy. This possibility is not lost on Tiger Woods or Sergio Garcia who both play with a standard-length driver.

Lie

While standard-length golf clubs will suit most golfers, the proper lie varies more among golfers. Ping was one of the first companies to recognize this and custom fit the buyers of their clubs for the correct lie. The lie is determined by the angle between the clubhead and the shaft when the club is soled flat on the ground. This lie angle is correct for you if, when you swing the club, the bottom of the sole of the club contacts the ground, not the toe or the heel. A lie that is either too upright or too flat will cause shots to fly left or right of the target, respectively (Figure 2.4). This effect of the lie of the club is greater with the short irons, which are shorter in length and have a more upright lie. The effect decreases as the length of the club increases and the lie angle decreases.

A simple, commonly used method for determining the proper lie is a static lie test. A static lie test involves simply taking your normal setup on a hard, flat surface and checking to see if the sole of the club (usually a 5-iron) rests flat on the surface. If the toe of the club does not touch the ground, the lie is too upright; if the heel does not touch the ground, the lie is too flat (Figure 2.4).

Fig. 2.4. Lie of the club and its effect on a golf shot.

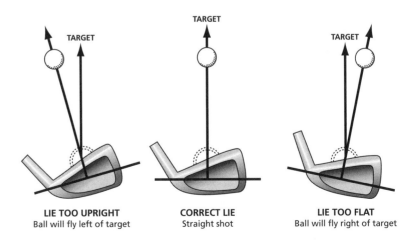

LIE TOO UPRIGHT
Ball will fly left of target

CORRECT LIE
Straight shot

LIE TOO FLAT
Ball will fly right of target

Fig. 2.5 Dynamic lie test.

A better, more preferred technique for determining if the lie is correct is a dynamic lie test. The dynamic lie test is accomplished by standing on a hard surface, swinging your club and contacting a hard plastic lie board. You would then make note of the mark left on the bottom of the sole of the club and where that mark is in relation to the center of the sole. If the mark is more toward the toe of the club, the lie is too flat. If the mark is more toward the heel, the lie is too upright. This method of fitting is more accurate and takes into account the downward bending of the shaft that occurs during the swing. If the mark is off-center (Figure 2.5), your club professional has a special tool to bend the hosel of the club to make the necessary correction.

Loft

The loft of the clubface is the angle in degrees between the center of the face and a vertical plane, which is perpendicular to the sole. The loft is set at the factory so that there is normally a 3° to 4° difference in the loft between each iron. This difference should be consistent to maintain a uniform progression in yardage and trajectory throughout the set. It is interesting to note that the old standard for loft used by the original equipment manufacturers no longer exists. A good example is the difference between the old standard and the current average loft for a 5-iron. The old standard (1960s) loft for a 5-iron was 32°. By the 1980s the average 5-iron had only 28° of loft, and today the average is down to 25°. Now we know that it is not just the ball that is contributing to the increased distance that golfers are hitting the ball. Today's 5-iron has the same loft as a 3-iron from the 1960s. The current industry average loft of clubs is illustrated in Figure 2.6.

When you purchase a new set of clubs it is recommended that you have the loft checked on each club, particularly if you have forged clubs. Forged clubs are made from softer steel than cast clubs and the loft can be easily corrected if it is off. Normally, you will get roughly a 10-yard difference in distance between each of your irons. When the loft on a club is incorrect it can have a significant effect on the yardage that you get from that club. If the loft is off on one or more of your clubs, it will make it difficult to judge the distance you will get from each club, thus making club selection from various distances very confusing.

The loft on the club affects the launch angle of the shot and creates backspin, which affects the trajectory of the shot and how far the ball will roll once it hits the ground. If your swing plane and angle of attack are correct, the more loft a club has, the higher the shot will fly. Increased backspin also reduces sidespin, helping the shot fly straighter. The relatively low loft of the driver and the long irons is a contributing factor, which makes it harder to get shots with these clubs airborne and to hit the shot straight. For this reason, as a beginner, you would be better off parking your driver and long irons (3- and 4-irons) in a closet at home, and instead, using your 3-wood for tee shots and your 7- and 9-woods in place of the 3 and 4-irons. The loft and lower center of gravity of the fairway woods assist in getting the ball airborne more easily,

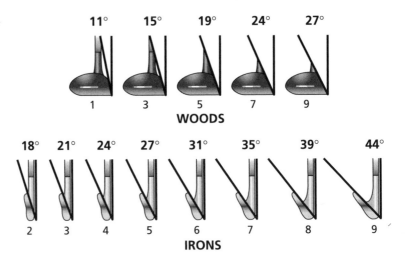

Fig. 2.6. Loft of woods and irons.

Fig. 2.7. Hybrid long irons.

providing more overall distance on the shot. The reduced sidespin makes it possible to hit straighter shots with fewer lost balls and fewer penalty strokes. Some manufacturers have actually begun to replace the 3- and 4-irons with a hybrid club that looks like a cross between an iron and a fairway wood (Figure 2.7).

Swing Weight

The swing weight of a club is a figure used to express the relationship of the weight of the clubhead, the shaft and the grip to the length of the club. This "weight" is important as it relates to how light or heavy the club "feels" as you hold it and as you swing it. Two clubs that actually weigh the same will feel heavier or lighter if their swing weights are different.

The swing weight of the club is denoted by a letter and number system. The letters A–E represent the heel-toe balance of the club, and the numbers 0–9 represent the overall weight on the swing weight scale. The higher the letter and number the heavier the club will feel at the head. Although swing weights range from B-0 to E-9, the swing weight of most clubs will fall in the C-8 to D-3 range for men and the C-3 to C-7 range for women. Most manufacturers assemble clubs with a swing weight of D-0. This swing weight remains constant throughout the set. This is accomplished by increasing the weight of the club head by 7 grams as the length of the shaft decreases by ½ inch. The difference between a club with a swing weight of D-0 and D-1 is only .07 ounces (the weight of a dime), and is almost unnoticeable when holding the two clubs. However, this difference is noticeable when you swing the clubs due to the centrifugal force on the clubhead.

The swing weight of the club is important in relation to your strength and endurance. If the swing weight of the club is too high you may not be able to generate maximum clubhead speed, and you may tire more easily during the round. This will adversely affect the control of your shots. If the swing weight is too low you will not have a good "feel" for the clubhead and may have difficulty making consistent contact in the sweet spot. Experimenting with different swing weights will allow you to find the swing weight that gives you the most consistent contact in the sweet spot of the clubface.

The new, lighter graphite shafts and titanium clubheads have allowed manufacturers to increase the size of clubheads without increasing the weight of the clubhead. This has also allowed them to lengthen the shaft without changing the swing weight. Golfers have benefited from these advances as a larger sweet spot makes the club more forgiving and a longer shaft produces more clubhead speed. Both of these factors—centeredness of contact and clubhead speed—create longer, straighter shots according to the ball flight laws

Grips

The last consideration in club selection is the grip (Figure 2.8). The main concerns when choosing a grip are material and grip size. Leather grips, the original material used for golf grips, have been almost completely replaced by rubber grips. Rubber grips are less expensive, less slippery, more durable, impervious to weather and easier to maintain than leather grips. Choose a grip that feels most comfortable to you. Grip size is important because a grip should feel comfortable in the hands of the golfer. Also, the size of the grip may influence the position of the clubface at impact.

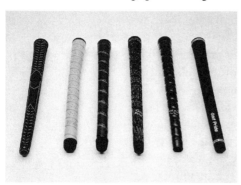

Fig. 2.8. Various golf grips.

Grips that are too small may contribute to overactive hands and a slightly closed clubface at contact with the ball. Grips that are too large may inhibit hand rotation, leaving the clubface open at contact with the ball. If the middle two fingers of the left hand (for right handed golfers) touch the pad of the thumb, the grip fits. Unless you have very large or small hands, or your fingers are very long or short, the standard size grip will fit the majority of golfers. The basic recommendation is to find a grip size that is both comfortable and allows you to consistently square the clubface at impact with the ball. In the past couple of years, grip manufacturers have begun to offer grips that are softer (spongier) in order to help absorb the shock of the club's impact with the ball. These grips are especially helpful for those with arthritic joints and/or those who are prone to golfers' (tennis) elbow.

Choosing a Putter

Your putter is your most important club. Remember, par for each hole allows for two putts, which means that up to 50 percent of your shots will be made with this one club. Putting is the most individual aspect of the game of golf. Putters and putting styles follow form in that almost no two are alike. Each club manufacturer offers several styles of putters (Figure 2.9), and each of the styles will have numerous variations. When choosing a putter, take your time and try several different putters before you make a final selection since this is the most important club in your bag. Dave Pelz (1995), one of the leading experts on putting and the short game, lists the following three factors as most important in selecting a putter:

1. length and lie
2. putter balance; and
3. the combination of head shape and alignment aids.

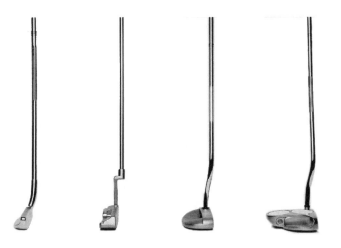

Fig. 2.9. Various putters.

Fig. 2.10. Long putters (left and right) and a belly putter (center).

The length and lie of your putter should compliment your individual physique and preferences so that you will be able to set-up to the putt with your eyes directly over the ball and with your hands directly under your shoulders. This position should also permit you to practice putting without undue back pain. Some golfers, especially senior golfers, have tried the long (approximately 52 inches) putter (Figure 2.10) to reduce back pain and/or improve their putting. In the last few years many golfer have tried a mid-length (approximately 42 inches), or "belly" putter. Pelz (2003), found through extensive testing that using the belly putter is the most accurate style of putting. If you have the opportunity to try one of the long putters and one of the belly putters on an outdoor putting green, you may find that you have more success with one of these longer putters. However, it is recommended that you do not purchase a putter based on the results of a few putts on one of the little artificial greens in a store.

The putter balance (sweet spot location and position of the shaft attachment) is important in minimizing twisting of the clubhead at impact, which produces directional errors. Center-shafted putters are best if you tend to mishit your putts toward the toe of the club, while heel-shafted putters are better if you tend to mishit toward the heel. The head shape and alignment aids (lines, arrows, etc.) etched or painted on the clubhead are important in helping to visualize the line of the putt and in aiming the clubhead properly.

The physical characteristics of the putter make up half of the equation. Your attitude and confidence level make up the other half. Former PGA Tour professional and current TV golf analyst Ken Venturi (1987) believes that confidence is the most important aspect of putting. Since confidence is such a big factor, it is important to make sure that your putter looks and feels just right to you. If you are second-guessing your choice of putters your negative thoughts will more or less doom you to wishing the ball in the hole. After you have decided on a putter, have your golf professional help you to double-check the length and lie to make sure that they are correct.

Golf Balls

After spending a considerable amount of time sorting through all of the variables in choosing a set of clubs and a putter that fit you, why not take just a little more time to find a golf ball that also fits your game? In the past 100 years, two kinds of golf balls have revolutionized the game, making the ball a preeminent part of the game. At the turn of the 20th century, the innovative Coburn Haskell took a thin strand of rubber which he wound around a rubber core and fashioned a gutta-percha cover for his new ball. This wound, 3-piece ball flew a good 20 yards further than the solid gutta percha ball of the time. Once the new Haskell ball hit the ground it also bounced and rolled farther than the solid gutta-percha ball. Because the Haskell ball was more difficult to control, many purists initially dismissed it; however, it didn't take long for golf professionals to realize the extra distance could be used to their advantage.

The pros were not the only ones to embrace the Haskell ball, however. The average golfer of that time was no different than today's golfers in that they were quick to jump on any product that could add distance to their shots. B. F. Goodrich Company was the first to begin mass production of the Haskell ball. Then Spalding Company made three important changes to the Haskell ball that made wound golf balls so popular. First, they began using a balata cover, which they found would adhere better to the rubber windings. Next, they produced the first cover for the ball that was actually white. Up until this time golf balls simply were painted white. Their third innovation that greatly improved golf ball performance was putting dimples (they bought the patent for dimples from William Taylor) on the cover of the ball (Peper, 1999). This was an improvement over the raised "bramble" pattern of golf ball covers that were in use at that time. Although improved on, this same basic type of golf ball design remained the choice of professionals throughout the 20th century.

Spalding, in the late 1960s, again provided the impetus for change in golf balls that would drive the wound 3-piece golf ball out of production. Spalding's 2-piece Top-Flite® ball began the revolution of solid-core golf balls that were less expensive and provided more distance than the wound ball. With its solid core and Surlyn cover, the Top-Flite® was also practically indestructible. While the wound ball, with its balata cover was easy to cut or crease with a mishit shot, the new Surlyn cover and solid core could "take a licking and keep on ticking." The 2-piece

*Fig. 2.11. Modern
solid core 3-piece ball
(right), and old
wound 3-piece ball
(left).*

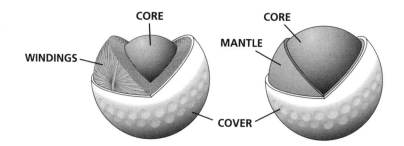

ball was also harder and flew farther than the wound ball. Another advantage of the harder 2-piece ball was the fact that it had a lower spin rate than the wound ball. A lower spin rate results in less side spin which produces a slice or a hook on miss hit shots. All of these factors (lower cost, more distance, increased durability and less slice or hook) made this type of ball a favorite for the average golfer. Professionals and more skilled golfers, however, preferred the wound ball because with its higher spin rate they could shape (curve) their shots better, and they had a much softer feel. They especially appreciated the soft feel of the wound ball on shots around the greens.

By the late 1990s, manufacturers were experimenting with new core materials and inner linings (called a mantle) for the solid-core balls turning some of them into 3- and 4-piece balls. This new mantle and cover, made from a urethane (Figure 2.11), allow for a larger, softer core and a much thinner, softer cover than the Surlyn covered 2-piece golf ball. These new 3-piece solid-core balls kept the advantages of the 2-piece ball (more distance and indestructible construction) while maintaining the softer feel of the wound ball. Now golfers have the best of both worlds in one golf ball. Titleist® was the last company that still manufactured wound 3-piece golf balls. Production ceased in 2002 due to the performance advantage and resulting popularity of their solid-core 3-piece Titleist® Pro V1 ball.

For most beginners, economics should play the major role in selecting a golf ball. Your best choice would be to buy less expensive golf balls until your game improves to the point that you can keep the ball in play more easily and are not losing balls as often. The worst ball on the market today is better than the best ball of 5 or 10 years ago. You may even want to consider playing with recycled golf balls (recovered from golf course water hazards), which will play just fine for the beginner. After you have more experience playing and you are able to make solid contact with the ball on a consistent basis, you may find that you prefer one type or brand of golf ball to the others.

Bags

When deciding which golf bag to purchase, the most important factor to consider, outside of economics, is whether you plan to carry your clubs, pull them on a cart, or ride in a golf cart. If you plan to walk and carry your clubs (the way the game was intended to be played), a smaller, lighter bag would be best. There are many bands and styles of bags, including some made of durable, lightweight materials that work nicely. The trend in carry bags today is to improve the ergonomics of the bag by using two shoulder straps, much like on a backpack, to balance the load and take stress off of the golfer's back (Figure 2.12). This innovation has made carrying your bag easier on your back, and makes it less tiring physically to carry your bag for 18 holes (5 plus miles). In addition, most carry bags today have collapsible legs that fold out when you set the bottom of the bag on the ground and fold in against the bag when you pick it up to carry it. This keeps the bag off of the ground allowing you easier access to your clubs and the pockets on the bag, and keep the bag and its contents clean and dry.

Pull/push carts (Figure 2.13) are popular with many golfers because they allow you to get the exercise and enjoyment of walking the course without having to shoulder the weight of the bag and clubs. Injuries and age eventually force many golfers to use a pull cart or ride an electric

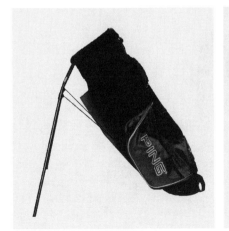

Fig. 2.12. (left) Carry bag with backpack type straps.

Fig. 2.13. (right) pull/push cart.

Fig. 2.14. Cart bag.

cart. Because you will be pulling or pushing the cart up, over and around the golf course you may want to use a light carry bag or find a light cart bag. "Cart" bags, which were recently introduced to the market, are designed specifically for those who ride in electric carts or those who use a pull cart (Figure 2.14). The differences in these bags from the old style bag is that most do not have a carry strap that just gets in the way, and all of the pockets are moved to the front and sides of the bag so that you have easy access to all of the pockets without having to take the bag off the cart. Cart bags tend to be larger and heavier than carry bags, but they do hold many more accessories.

Accessories

The list of accessories and novelties that you might choose to purchase is too numerous to detail, but some of the more important or useful accessories (Figure 2.15) include:

Fig. 2.15. Accessories.

1. **Shoes** – most golf shoes have replaceable, soft rubber spikes on the soles that provide better traction so that your feet do not slip while swinging a club, and so that you do not slip on wet grass or steep terrain. Shoes with metal spikes are no longer acceptable. Almost every course in the United States has banned metal spikes because they can track fungus and diseases onto the putting green that are harmful to the grass. Metal spikes are also more destructive to the surface of the green. A big plus for golf shoes over street shoes or tennis shoes is that most new golf shoes are waterproof. Nothing ruins the pleasure of a round of golf quicker than getting your feet wet before you have even finished the first hole. Be sure to put shoe trees in your shoes after each round so that they will dry more effectively and retain their shape. This will help them to be more comfortable and last much longer.

2. **Glove** – usually worn on the left hand of right-handed golfers to help protect the hand from blisters and to help keep the club from slipping if the grip gets wet from sweat or rain. Be sure to ask your golf professional to help you find the correct fit.

3. **Tees** – wooden or plastic pegs used to elevate (tee) the ball on the first shot (tee shot) of each hole. This handy device is only about 100 years old. Prior to the late 1800s, tee shots were made by placing the ball on a small mound made from sand or dirt.

4. **Ball mark repair tool** – to keep the greens smoother and the game more enjoyable. If you repair your ball mark as soon as you get to the green, the grass will heal in about 2 or 3 days. If left for a few hours it will take 2 or 3 weeks for the grass to heal.

5. **Head covers** – made from a soft material to cover your woods and protect their finish. Those who ride in a cart need the protection of head covers more because the clubs are bouncing around and banging into each other as the cart moves over the rough terrain of the golf course. If you have graphite shafts on your clubs it is better to use head covers that have a long neck to protect the shaft from rubbing on the edge of the bag. This rubbing will take the paint off of the shaft, and will eventually leave a groove in the shaft.

6. **Towel** – to dry your hands and face in the heat or rain, and to clean the golf clubs so that the scoring lines on the club can do their job.

7. **Umbrella and rain gear** – even though "it does not rain on the golf course!"
8. **Ball retriever** – for that occasional ball that strays into a water hazard.
9. **First aid kit** – sunscreen, band-aids, bug repellent, bee sting swabs, etc.
10. **USGA Rule Book** – "Don't leave home without it."
11. **Instructional books and videos** – to increase your understanding of the game and improve your swing.

Care of Equipment

With a minimum amount of care and maintenance, your golf equipment should serve you well for many years. There is no reason not to expect your clubs to last 20 years or more. Cleaning your clubs regularly will help them to last longer and allow them to do their job properly. The grooves in your woods and irons were designed to help put spin on the ball; however, when clogged with dirt or grass, they cannot serve this function. It is best to use your towel after each shot to clean your clubs. As a minimum, use some warm soapy water and a soft brush to clean your clubs after each round.

The grips of your clubs are often more neglected than the heads of the clubs. Dirt, sweat, and oil from your hands will accumulate if the grips are not cleaned periodically. Warm soapy water and a washcloth do a great job. Also, replacing the grips every year will add that "like-new" feel to your clubs.

Your glove and shoes should not be overlooked if you expect them to look nice and to have a longer life. Your shoes will also be more comfortable if you put shoetrees in them and allow them to dry between rounds. Applying shoe polish on a regular basis will help to prevent them from cracking and splitting. By replacing your spikes periodically, you can help to avoid slips and maintain consistent footing from round to round.

Golf balls, clubs, shoes, etc. do not hold up well under extreme changes of temperature. When storing your golf clubs and equipment at home, find a closet or room in your house rather than putting them in the attic or garage. When transporting your clubs to and from the golf course the interior or trunk of your car is a fine place to put them, but it is not recommended for long-term storage. The temperature extremes in your attic, garage or car trunk will only contribute to the premature demise (e.g., cause the grips to harden and become slippery) of your golf clubs and other equipment. This is especially important for graphite shafts, since high temperatures may damage the fibers. Also, leaving golf balls in the trunk for extended periods will adversely affect their performance.

3 Pre-Swing Fundamentals

The Foundation

The foundation of your golf game will be your ability to establish fundamentally sound habits in preparing to swing the golf club and in making contact with the ball. "Address," the position you assume prior to starting your swing, will include three distinct parts: (1) grip—or hold on the club; (2) alignment—the aiming process; and (3) set-up—your stance and posture. A proper grip, correct alignment, and a natural athletic setup, are the building blocks—the pre-swing fundamentals—upon which a solid golf swing must first be developed. By providing yourself with a habitually sound address position—by repeating these basic fundamentals—there will be an increased likelihood that a good swing and a good shot will be the result.

Choosing a Grip

The purpose of the grip is to balance the strength of the two hands by coupling them into a working unit. Since the hands are the only contact that you have with the club, the turn of the body away from and back into the ball must be timed through the action of the hands. Early in golf's history, players used the 10-finger grip (Figure 3.1) until Harry Vardon, the great English champion, popularized the overlapping grip (Figure 3.2) in the early 1920s. This grip won wide-spread acceptance and has been used by the majority of players since. A third commonly used grip is called the interlocking grip (Figure 3.3). The selection of the best grip for you is not a science but a choice dictated by individual preferences.

Research varies on the percentages of players using the three most common methods of holding the golf club.

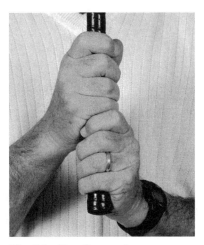

Fig. 3.1. Ten-finger grip.

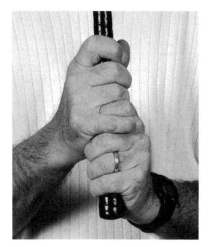

Fig. 3.2. Overlapping grip.

Fig. 3.3. Interlocking grip.

About 70 percent of all golfers use the overlapping style. About 20 percent use the interlocking and another 10 percent use the 10-finger grip. Approximately 1 percent use some other method of holding the club, such as the Australian grip where the target hand thumb is not inside, but outside, the dominant hand position. The size and the strength of the hands and fingers are the primary factors in the selection of the grip. Players with normal strength and hand size usually select the overlapping grip. The interlocking grip is preferred by players with small hands or short fingers, while the 10-finger grip is often chosen by those with less than average hand strength. Youngsters just starting out in golf or seniors learning golf for the first time are often good candidates for a 10-finger grip. Unfortunately, many beginners start with a faulty grip and find it difficult to change. Check with a golf professional or your golf instructor to make sure that you correct any flaws in your hand positioning early in your golf career.

In all discussions within this text, we have made every attempt to be aware of differences in hand dominance among our readers. To make the terminology applicable to you regardless of your "handedness," these terms need to be defined: target hand (or target side)—that hand or part of your body closer to the intended target, dominant hand (or dominant side)—that hand or part of your body farther from the target. Most righthanders address the ball with their right or dominant hand farther from the target; by the same token, lefthanders would find their strong hand, the left, farther from the target.

Holding the Club with Your Target Hand

1. Extend the target hand so that the club's grip lies across the middle section of the index finger and back across the palm near the base of the little finger. The grip should run on a diagonal, from under the heel pad of your target hand, and extend through the first and second joints of your index finger (Figure 3.4).

2. Curl your index finger lightly around the club, lift the club up in front of your target hip. The weight of the club should be felt under the heel pad and on the first two joints of the index finger (Figure 3.5).

3. Place the club head on the ground—the "soled" position—and wrap your fingers around the grip with your thumb positioned right of center for a righthander, left of center for a lefthander (Figure 3.6).

4. Have a small portion of the butt end of the club visible, so that the heel of your hand does not contact the end of the grip.

Fig. 3.4. Target hand finger position.

Holding the Club with Your Dominant Hand

1. Place your dominant hand on the club so that the club's grip lies across the middle part of the index finger and rests primarily at the base of your fingers. The palm of your dominant hand should not be in contact with the golf club (Figure 3.7).

Fig. 3.5. Target hand heel pad position.

2. Close your fingers around the club with the little finger of the dominant hand lying on top of the area between the index and middle fingers of the target hand. This is called the overlap grip. In the interlocking grip, the little finger of the dominant hand interlocks between the index and middle fingers of the target hand. The 10-finger grip has the little finger of the dominant hand touching or side by side with the index finger of the target hand.

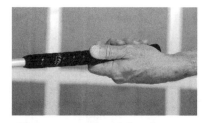

Fig. 3.6. Target hand thumb position.

3. In all grip types the dominant thumb should be positioned left of center for a righthander, right of center for a lefthander.

Grip Pressure

How much grip pressure is necessary? Without question, excessive pressure can tighten the muscles of the forearms and restrict the smooth flow of the swing,

Fig. 3.7. Dominant hand finger position.

thereby decreasing clubhead speed and prohibiting the squaring of the clubface at contact with the ball. Another concern is the change in grip pressure from the start of the swing through to the finish, which most commonly occurs during the transition from the back swing to the forward swing. Golf instructors often attempt to explain grip pressure by using examples to which students can relate. If you were to ask ten golf teachers to explain the correct grip pressure, they would likely use ten different analogies. The three that are most often used to describe the correct amount of grip pressure are listed below:

1. Squeezing toothpaste out of a tube smoothly; excessive pressure would forcefully squirt it out.
2. Holding a bird in your hands; do not let the bird fly away yet do not hurt it.
3. Hold the golf club with the same amount of pressure you would hold a pencil.

Checkpoints – Target Hand

1. The thumb should be slightly to the rear of the center of the shaft.
2. The knuckles of the index and middle finger should be visible.
3. The back of your hand should face the target.
4. Pressure on the club should be provided by the last three fingers of your hand (little, ring, and middle fingers).

Checkpoints – Dominant Hand

1. The inverted V formed by your thumb and index finger should point to a spot between your chin and shoulder on that side of your body (Figure 3.8).
2. The thumb should be slightly to the target side of the center of the shaft.
3. The knuckles of the index finger and possibly the middle finger should be visible.
4. The palm of that hand should be facing the target.
5. The club should be in the base of the fingers, not in contact with the palm.

Fig. 3.8. Correct grip.

Checkpoint – Both Hands

The palms of your hands should be opposite (facing) one another, so that they may work together as a single unit.

Alignment

The foundation for the alignment process is the target line, which is the imaginary line from the target to the ball. Before assuming your stance in preparing to make your swing, stand behind the ball, keeping the intended target in view. Pick out a spot (a piece of grass, a discoloration, a broken tee) one to two feet in front of the ball to use as a more specific target. This short-sight alignment aid (Figure 3.9) or intermediate target, is much easier to align with than is the intended target, which may be as much as 200 hundred yards away and nearly abstract in its lack of definition. When the address position is assumed, which will include the grip, alignment, and set-up, special attention is given to the alignment process. At address, a line drawn across your toes (more accurately a line connecting the heels of your feet but harder to see) should be parallel to your target line (Figure 3.10). First place a club

Fig. 3.9. (left) Visualizing the target line.

Fig. 3.10. (right) Toe line parallel to target line at address.

Fig. 3.11. A club held across the thighs and the shoulders should be parallel to the target line.

across both thighs, then across the front of your shoulders, in both instances the club should be parallel to your target line (Figure 3.11).

You now have one of two choices in aligning your golf club to the intended target. The first is to hold the club in your hands with the correct grip, with the club extended in front of you and the toe of the club pointing to the sky. The scoring lines, those parallel lines or grooves etched in the clubface, should be perpendicular to the ground and aligned to your midsection. At address, the golf club is then positioned behind the ball so that the scoring lines are perpendicular to or at right angles to your target line. The second choice is to place your golf club behind the golf ball, again at a right angle to the target line, and assume your stance around that position which would include correctly positioning your hands. Either method is correct, the important point is that you have a method in aligning your clubface to the target line giving yourself the best opportunity to execute a successful shot. To perhaps help you in visualizing the alignment process, you will have created the shape of an "H" with your imaged lines at address (Figure 3.12). The primary line is the target line, a line parallel to that is across your toes (often called the "foot" line), and a connecting line between them is defined by the scoring lines on your clubface. Golfers have to spend a great deal of practice time with the alignment process, to the point that it becomes habitual, a part of your routine.

Set-Up

Your stance for the full swing is made by placing your feet at right angles to your target line. For most full swing shots, your feet will usually be about shoulder width apart. For best ball placement, most golfers prefer to stand so that the ball is placed approximately two inches inside the target heel. Ball placement should actually be determined by where your golf swing reaches its bottommost point during the forward swing. However, as a beginner, you may find more success by placing the ball at the center of your stance. As you gain swing efficiency, primarily in respect to weight transfer to the target foot, the ball location can be moved forward toward the target heel. Use the crosspiece of your aligning "H" to aid you in finding the best ball position, or lay some irons on the ground in the shape of an "H" to help make this process more vivid (Figure. 3.12).

Fig. 3.12. Using clubs to help align your stance.

Your set-up posture should be natural and balanced. Your knees will have a small amount of flex and by bending forward at the hips, your buttocks will be extended back behind you. Accomplishing this will tilt your back (spine) forward toward the ball, thereby allowing an inclined angle to be created between the ground and your upper body. As you stand in this address posture, your arms should hang comfortably from the shoulders, perpendicular to the ground. In this position, your hands (actually the butt end of your club) will be approximately 4-6 inches (the width of your fist) from your thighs (Figure 3.13).

The weight on your feet should be evenly distributed and between your heels and toes. Most golf teachers refer to this as an athletic position, one similar to playing shortstop in baseball, guarding an opponent in basketball, or receiving a serve in tennis. The target foot should be

Fig. 3.13. Side view of a correct stance.

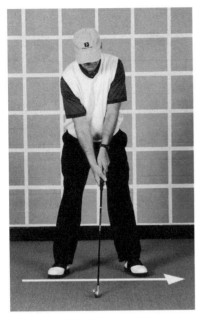

Fig. 3.14. Front view of a correct stance.

turned slightly outward towards the target and the dominant foot should be almost at a right angle to the target line (Figure 3.14). In instances when flexibility is lacking, turn the dominant foot out away from the target slightly to allow upper body rotation to take place.

Beginning players are often confused about how far they should stand from the ball and how far the hands should hang from the body. The different distances within the set-up are affected by a person's size as well as by the club being used. For example, taller players will generally be closer to the ball than heavy-set players. In addition, the differences in length and lie between dissimilar clubs requires an adjustment in the player's proximity to the ball. Overall, golfers should attempt to find a comfortable position for their arms to hang from their body, striving for a feeling of comfort, with no feeling of reaching out for the ball. After all of this and to remain relaxed prior to initiating the swing, consider including a "waggle," a small movement of the club away from and back to the ball as a means of reducing tension in arms and shoulders.

The importance of developing a routine before each shot cannot be overemphasized. Consistency in this pre-shot routine greatly increases your chances for success.

Checkpoints – Pre-Shot Routine

1. Sight down the target line from behind the ball, visualizing the shot you want to hit, and pick out an intermediate target some 12" to 24" in front of the ball.
2. Place the clubhead behind the ball, squaring the clubface to your target line (Figure 3.15).
3. Take the proper grip. (Remember that #2 and #3 can be in reverse order).
4. With your feet close together, imagine a line from the ball to your feet which is perpendicular to the target line. Remember the crosspiece of the "H" (Figure 3.16).
5. Take a short step with your target foot and then a larger step with your dominant foot (Figure 3.17).
6. Waggle.
7. Refocus on your target, then swing.

Fig. 3.15. Squaring the clubface to the target line.

Fig. 3.16. Feet centered on the ball, square to the target line.

Fig. 3.17. Stance correctly aligned on the target line and the ball.

4 Swing Fundamentals

The professional golfers you may have watched during televised golf tournaments have developed swings that are successful for them only after years of practice and competition. You will have seen a variety of swings among those players due to their physical differences and personal preferences. What you will see in the golf swings of all great players are certain characteristics that beginning golfers should try to incorporate into their own swings.

A great deal of time has been spent over the years analyzing the golf swing. And because it is such a fascinating subject, those efforts spent at analyzing are not expected to change during your lifetime. The best advice for you is to make the swing as simply constructed in your mind as you possibly can. Try to avoid getting bogged down with what every small muscle or body part is doing or should be doing during your swing. Instead think of the major, or big muscles doing the work—kind of like a dog and its tail. We want to avoid having the tail wag the dog.

Fig. 4.1. The swing triangle.

The Swing Triangle

After mastering (or at least establishing) the pre-swing fundamentals at the address position, you should spend a considerable amount of time working on the swing components covered in this chapter. At address, imagine that you have created a triangle which extends from your target hand, to your target shoulder, across your shoulder girdle to your dominant shoulder, and then on down to your dominant hand. The line across your shoulders forms the base of this triangle. The altitude of the triangle is represented by the distance from your sternum to your hands, which forms one of the vertices of the triangle (Figure 4.1). Establishing this triangle prior to all of your shots will give you a greater opportunity for success. The shape of the triangle may be altered slightly for some of your shot-making (the chip shot perhaps), but the concept of utilizing the triangle to initiate the swing motion is recognized by most golf teachers as a sound beginning.

Backswing

The process of beginning the backswing, i.e., moving the clubhead away from the ball, has been labeled as the "takeaway" portion of the

backswing. That term connotes the use of the dominant side to cause the action in picking up or elevating the golf club, which contradicts what should actually happen. The preferred method would be to move your swing triangle away from the ball as though that triangle was of one-piece construction. The prime movers in this case would be the major muscle groups in your back and shoulders, i.e. those which form the base portion of your imagined triangle. That triangle should move as a single unit in a sweeping motion away from the ball until your hands—and the clubhead as an extension of your hands—reach about a seven o'clock position on a clock face. Your head would be at twelve o'clock and your feet would be at six (Figure 4.2). If you initiate your backswing by turning or rotating your shoulders instead of emphasizing your hands or arms as the principle movers, you will find

Fig. 4.2. One piece takeaway.

greater consistency in your swing, and you will more easily achieve and maintain a natural tempo.

Once the backswing has begun, simply turn your back to the target by continuing to rotate your shoulders, while keeping your head in a position similar to where it was at address. Your head may even travel a short distance away from the target. If you can rotate so that the line across your shoulders—the base of your swing triangle—is at a right angle to the target line, you will find it relatively easy for your hands to get to a shoulder-high position. Do not be concerned with where or whether your hands hinge on the backswing. Providing that you have retained that light grip pressure established at address, your hands should flex or hinge automatically as a result of the load or weight of the club.

The foundation you created at address with your setup becomes extremely important now. As you reach the top of your backswing, you will find that you have transferred as much as 60–65% of your weight to your dominant foot. That weight should be located on the inside portion of your dominant foot and toward its heel (Figure 4.3). It is essential that you maintain your weight within the address foundation you created earlier during the pre-swing fundamentals. It is a common fault among beginners for their body weight to sway during the backswing to a point outside the address foundation. This shift beyond the back edge of the dominant shoe will negate the prospects of a good weight shift through the ball and a consistently sound swing. The crossed arms drill (Chapter 9, Figures 9.4, 9.5, 9.6) will give you a good indication of what the swing will feel like and is an excellent drill for gaining a kinesthetic awareness for weight transfer within your foundation.

Fig. 4.3. Top of the backswing.

Backswing Checkpoints

The first checkpoint that occurs during the backswing is labeled the "¼ swing position." That ¼ swing position occurs when the shaft of the club becomes parallel to the ground and is also parallel to the target line. There are three parameters that should be in place at this checkpoint. The first is that the club's scoring lines should be perpendicular to the ground. Secondly, the altitude of the swing triangle should be the same as it was at the start of the swing. In other words, you have maintained the length of swing lever you established at address. The length of that lever is best represented by the distance from your hands to your sternum, although others may suggest that your target arm maintains the lever created at address. Third and finally, your dominant elbow will be pointing to the ground or to your dominant hip, whichever is easiest for you to visualize.

Fig. 4.4. ¼ swing checkpoint.

With practice, you should be able to swing to this checkpoint position and find all three parameters in place: (1) scoring lines perpendicular to the ground; (2) lever length maintained; and (3) the dominant elbow in a passive position (Figure 4.4). In fact, an excellent drill is to stand in front of a full-length mirror; assume an address posture, close your eyes and try to duplicate the ¼ swing position. Then, open your eyes to see whether or not you were successful in recreating this checkpoint. Through practice you can develop the "feel" for the golf club's position in space and the repetitions experienced through practicing will allow this ¼ swing checkpoint to become a part of your overall swing blueprint. The ¼ swing checkpoint, by the way, is a swing position utilized in your short game—a great reason for another chapter in this text—so you are in fact practicing a skill to be used on the golf course.

The second checkpoint is at the ¾ backswing position. Here, the hands should be approximately shoulder high and the golf club position will be nearly vertical—depending on your body type and degree of flexibility. There are three checkpoint parameters at this position: (1) body weight should be shifted to the dominant foot and heel; (2) the swing lever created at address is maintained; and (3) the dominant elbow should still be passive, pointing to the ground or to the hip in what may be referred to as a load-carrying position (Figure 4.5). There are other parameters you can look at closely in the ¾ position, but they will be of less influence than the primary three. One of these is that the target hand, wrist and forearm should be in a fairly straight line, not cupped (concave) nor bowed outward (convex). Any hand flexion that does occur should appear at the base of the target thumb, not on the back of the hand.

Fig. 4.5. ¾ backswing checkpoint.

Forward Swing

The forward swing is merely going from a "back to the target" position to a "stomach to the target " position using the big muscles in your legs, back and shoulders. A number of things are taking place during the forward swing or the downswing. Weight is being transferred toward the target side. You are rotating around your body's center, a point located near to or slightly lower than your sternum. Interrelated to the rotation and transfer of weight, it is widely held that the leg muscles are the prime movers in the initial stages of the downswing. Additionally, you should strive to maintain nearly the same head position that was established at address until well after contact with the ball has occurred. Following all of this, try to allow your body to move freely and naturally during the forward swing, avoid thinking about it—it should not be a cognitive process. At this point in time, please note that the word "hit" has not been used to describe the golf swing.

Finish

The end of your swing is called the "finish," or what may be referred to as the follow-through. Your finish should involve three specific body parts: elbows, navel, and dominant knee. At the finish, your elbows should be at shoulder height or higher to insure that you have extended through the golf ball's impact area during the swing. As aging occurs and flexibility decreases, getting your hands to that shoulder-high position may be all that you can accomplish. Secondly, your navel should point at the target. As swing efficiency is gained through effective rotation of the large muscles, your navel may point as much as ten degrees past the target. A good check-off item for those with sound golf swings is to make sure that your dominant shoulder is closer to the target than is your target shoulder. And thirdly, your dominant knee should point directly to the target. To reach this position, all of your body weight will have to transfer to your target foot and your dominant foot will move to where only the toe of your shoe will be in contact with the ground, maintaining a balanced position (Figure 4.6). In the finish position, if your elbows are shoulder height and your navel and dominant knee are pointing at the target, you will have done most things correctly en route to the finish—providing that you are on balance when you reach this point. Balance is an essential ingredient in your swing, and it must be maintained throughout the swing, even to the finish. You are encouraged to hold your finish position for a few seconds as you watch the ball fly down the middle of the fairway.

Fig. 4.6. Finish position.

Swing Tempo

The tempo or pace of your swing should reflect how you do things normally, i.e., how you walk, talk and move. If it is a natural extension of the way you do "stuff" then it will be much easier to consistently replicate. If, however, your swing tempo is manufactured or contrived and is not a natural way for you to swing, consistency will be elusive at best. The effort you expend during the downswing should be accelerating and should be something less than the maximum you can generate. Most teachers of golf recommend that the perceived effort of the swing be only about 75% of maximum. In other words, as you reach the top of your backswing, you are effectively at zero mph prior to starting the forward swing. As the downswing begins, it should be a gradually accelerating motion, reaching its

Figs. 4.7–4.9. Three views of the swing sequence.

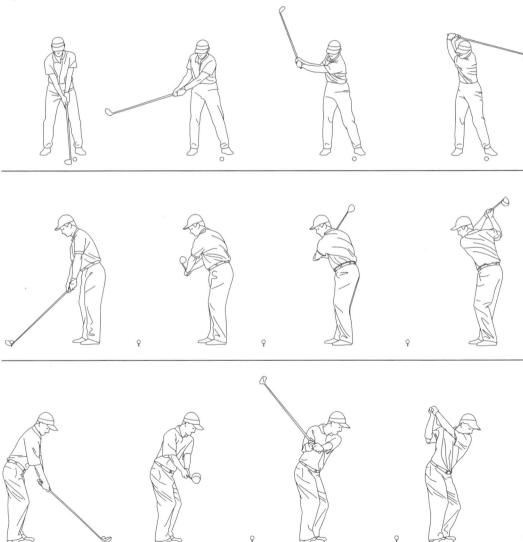

full—but less than maximum—speed just prior to impact with the golf ball and extending through the ball into a fundamentally solid "finish" position.

In conclusion, your golf swing focal point should be directed to a specific spot—a target—on the golf course where you want the ball to end up. The swing therefore becomes the vehicle to accomplish that, you are *swinging* towards a target, not *hitting* at a golf ball.

5 Irons and Woods

In the previous chapters you were introduced to the fundamentals of the pre-swing and the full swing. These fundamentals hold true regardless of which club you select when you are making a full swing. Every golf club is just a golf club, and you swing them all in the same manner. There is an old saying among golf instructors that "there is no one swing for every golfer, but every golfer has to have one swing." The reason for carrying 14 different clubs is to allow yourself one swing, yet be able to hit shots that have different distances, trajectories and spin objectives. It stands to reason that if the golf swing is at times difficult to master, then trying to master 14 different swings would be almost impossible.

It is the desire to hit the ball greater distances (especially with the driver) and to get the ball airborne that causes beginners and high-handicap golfers to hit so many poor shots. Rather than using the same swing they practiced so diligently and trusting the different clubs to do the work for them, they try to produce more distance by swinging harder or try to get the ball airborne by attempting to lift it. This chapter will focus on the pre-swing adjustments that should be made when making full swings with the different clubs so that the basic swing does not have to be altered.

Irons

The irons provide an infinite number of options relating to distance, trajectory and spin that affect how far the ball rolls after it hits the ground. These options exist because of the differences in the clubs themselves, not because of swing changes. The primary changes that you need to consider are the width of your stance and the position of the ball in your stance. The longer the shaft of the club (the lower the number of the club, e.g. a 2-iron vs. a 9-iron), the wider your stance needs to be in order to support a longer swing arc. The position of the ball in your stance should be 2–4 inches inside your target heel.

Fig. 5.1. Addressing the ball with a 3-iron.

Fig. 5.2. Addressing the ball with a pitching wedge.

If you determine the ball position in relationship to your target heel, it is much easier to be consistent in your pre-swing routine. Although it appears that the ball position is changed as different clubs are used (with a pitching wedge, the ball appears to be in the center of the stance, while with a 2-iron it appears to be closer to the target foot), this is not the case. In reality, the difference is actually due to the change in the width of your stance for the various clubs. As has been previously stated, for the beginner it may be advisable to place the ball in the center of your stance until you gain swing efficiency.

Two additional adjustments that are made depending on the iron used are the distance that you stand from the ball and your swing plane. These two adjustments are automatically made by the iron that you have selected. As you sole the club flat on the ground, the length of the shaft will move you the correct distance from the ball, while the lie of the club will make any minute adjustment that is necessary in your swing plane (Figures 5.1 and 5.2).

The shorter shaft, more upright lie and more narrow stance that are characteristic of the shorter irons produce a more upright swing plane. This upright swing plane produces a steeper angle of attack which allows you to make contact with the ball and take a nice divot just in front of the ball. The angle of attack (see ball flight laws, Chapter 7) and the loft on the clubface are what cause the ball to become airborne (do you remember Newton's third law of motion—every action has an equal and opposite reaction?), rather than an effort on your part to lift the ball into the air. Any deliberate attempt to get the ball airborne usually produces the opposite result. In attempting to lift the ball, your swing plane and the bottom of your swing arc are altered, causing many topped or "thin" shots—in which the ball contacts the club low on the face (on the first one or two scoring lines), or even on the leading edge of the blade.

Fairway Metalwoods

The fairway metalwoods are some of the least used clubs in a round of golf. Most par-3 and par-4 holes do not require them, and most courses do not have more than four par-5 holes. Therefore, you would not hit a fairway metalwood more than four or five times in a typical round. Also, how many practice shots do you hit with your fairway metalwoods? The lack of practice, the desire to get more distance, and the need to get the ball airborne from a fairway lie all conspire to make fairway metalwoods the club most feared by beginners and high handicappers.

By making three pre-swing adjustments you can improve your fairway metalwood shots tremendously. First, hit more practice shots with these clubs. You cannot do well that which you do not practice. Second, position the ball back from your target heel 2–4 inches (as you do for your iron shots) so that the club reaches the bottom of the swing arc as you make contact with the ball, thus sweeping the ball off the grass and taking only a very shallow divot (Figure 5.3). The shot is more like a long iron shot than a tee shot. Finally, the visual feedback you get when you are 200+ yards from the green versus 100 yards causes your brain to automatically think that you have to swing harder. You need to fight this instinct by playing a trick on yourself. The next time you are faced with a long fairway shot (metalwood or iron) think about your favorite club and how easily you swing that club to get the distance and trajectory you need. Then pretend that you are swinging this favorite club, making the same easy, effortless swing. You will be amazed at how much more distance and consistency you will begin to get on these longer shots.

Fig. 5.3. Fairway metal set-up.

Specialty Metalwoods

During the past few years, golf equipment manufacturers have started producing a wide variety of specialty metalwoods designed to make it easier to hit from the rough and to get fairway shots airborne more easily than with long irons. Originally these specialty metalwoods had the loft of a 5-wood (21°) and built up ridges or "rails" on the bottom to allow them to glide through the rough rather than digging into the ground. Now these metalwood clubs have evolved into distinct categories (7-wood, 9-wood, etc.) and commonly feature a shallow-face design. These clubs have gained wide acceptance among golfers not only for their ability to play shots from bad lies, but also because golfers found that they could hit better fairway shots (higher and longer) than they could with their long irons.

Drivers

Distance, or "how far can I make my tee shot go?" is the test the majority of golfers use to measure their prowess. Golfers have become obsessed with distance, and some of this obsession is due to the exposure that long-ball hitters like John Daly, Davis Love III, and Tiger Woods get on televised golf tournaments. The golf ball and club manufacturers prey on this obsession with promises of more distance if you will just buy their brand of ball or club. Beyond equipment changes (such as a longer shaft or a different shaft flex), you develop clubhead speed not by "hitting at" the ball or swinging the club harder with your dominant hand or by hitting from the top of your backswing. Instead, clubhead speed comes from making a normal, well-timed swing so that power and speed are delivered smoothly from the ground up. The principle that the basics of the swing are the same regardless of the club remains the same. Consistency and control are much more important than distance if you want to lower your golf score. In the words of the great golf instructor, Harvey Penick, "the woods are full of long drivers!" (Penick, 1992, p. 29).

The Tee Shot

The tee shot is the favorite shot of many golfers. The fact that the ball is teed up makes it one of the easiest shots to make, and the ball normally goes farther when hit from a tee. Unless you are playing a par-3 hole, the driver is the normal club most golfers use when hitting their tee shot. A driver, in the hands of a skilled player, will make the ball go farther than any club in the bag, but that does not always make it the best choice of clubs for your tee shot. As mentioned earlier, along with distance, getting the ball airborne is of greatest concern to most beginners and high handicap golfers. The lack of loft (7°–12°) on the face of a driver makes it difficult to get the shot airborne. And obviously, if you cannot get the ball airborne, it will not go as far. From a playability standpoint, a better choice of clubs for beginners would be a 3-metal when hitting a tee shot. The increased loft (approximately 16°) of this club and its slightly shorter shaft will increase your chances of not only hitting the ball farther, but also of hitting it straighter. A cardinal rule in golf is to put the ball in play!

When teeing the ball to hit your tee shot with a driver, you would like to have about one-third of the ball appearing above the top of the club-face. This rule of thumb may require some modification, i.e., higher ball height, if you are using a "wood" wood. To adjust for the trajectory of your shot, simply tee the ball lower if it is flying too high or tee it higher if it is flying too low. Because of the length and lie of the driver, the tee shot appears to be much like sweeping the ball off the tee rather than swinging down through the ball. To accomplish this, you should widen your stance slightly and adjust the position of the ball to a point even with the heel of your target foot (Figure 5.4). With the advent of over-length drivers, many of the better players are positioning the ball off their target foot instep, and some are even aligning the ball off the toe of their target foot—all due to the longer swing arc. The idea is to sweep the ball off the tee, making contact with the ball just after the club has reached the bottom of the swing arc and is starting to move up towards the finish. This provides a good launch angle and enhances overspin, which helps to increase the amount of roll once the ball hits the ground.

Fig. 5.4. Set-up for a tee shot.

6 The Short Game

In golf, your score is dependent on your skills in the "short game." Harvey Penick referred to the short game as "the magic words." The real magic is that improving your short game provides you with the best and fastest way to lower your scores. After studying golfers of all ability levels over the last 25 years (Pelz, 1999), found that almost two-thirds of the shots in a typical 18-hole round of golf fall within the short game. The short game begins for most golfers when they are within 80–100 yards of the green and includes pitch shots, chip shots and putts. Striking the ball well from the tee and the fairway gives you the opportunity to score well if you have a good short game. On those days when your timing is off and you are not striking the ball as well, a good short game can help you to avoid a high score.

The pitch shot, chip shot and putt differ in the length of the swing, the amount of time the ball spends in the air and the amount of time the ball spends rolling on the green. The pitch shot is generally the longest and most dramatic of the three shots, with a soft, high trajectory that lands the ball on the green about halfway to the hole. The pitch shot has more backspin, and its higher trajectory lands the ball on the green more softly with less roll. This type of shot is ideal when the ball must carry over obstacles near the green such as water, sand, severe undulations or even trees. However, a pitch shot is a low percentage shot because it is hard to predict how much backspin the shot will have or how the ball will react once it hits the green.

The chip shot, with its shorter, one-lever swing, is much simpler to execute, and the outcome is more predictable. A chip is almost like a putting stroke with an iron. It pops the ball up in the air on a low trajectory and lands it two or three feet on the green. The ball then rolls the rest of the way to the hole like a putt.

The putt is the easiest of the three shots because it requires the shortest, simplest swing and the ball stays on the ground the entire way to the hole. Although usually putts are made on the green, you can putt from off the edge of the green if the grass surrounding the green is short and even. In this case, a bad putt may end up closer to the hole than a good chip for a beginner.

Pitch Shots

Club Selection

Fig. 6.1. Loft and bounce.

PITCHING
WEDGE

48°

Minimal bounce: 2° - 5°

SAND WEDGE

56°

Lots of bounce: 10° - 16°

LOB WEDGE

60°

Minimal bounce: 0° - 10°

Possible club choices for a pitch shot normally include the pitching wedge, the sand wedge and the lob wedge. Some factors you want to consider are: the type of lie you find your ball in, the distance to the green and how much green you have to work with between the edge of the green and the hole. Of the three wedges (Figure 6.1), the pitching wedge (PW) will have the least amount of loft, about 48°, producing the lowest ball flight trajectory and potentially the most roll after the ball hits the green. It is a good choice from the fairway or the rough. The sand wedge (SW) normally has 56° of loft, which produces a shot with a slightly higher trajectory and less roll than the pitching wedge. Because of its heavy flange construction and high degree of bounce (how far, in degrees, the trailing edge of the sole extends below the leading edge of the clubface), the sand wedge is a good choice when hitting from heavy rough or long grass around the green. The lob wedge (LW) has about 60° of loft but less bounce than the sand wedge. Because of its high loft and low bounce, the lob wedge is a good choice from the fairway or from tight lies, where there is very little or no grass under the ball. The lob wedge will produce shots with a higher trajectory, a softer landing on the green and very little roll (Figure 6.2). You will learn through practice and experience how long your swing must be, how high you want the shot to fly and how close you need to land the ball to the hole—all factors in deciding which club to use.

The Grip

For pitch shots use the same grip that you use for your full swing. Grip pressure should be light so that your hands and arms stay soft and relaxed, allowing you to sense the length and speed of the swing and to

Fig. 6.2. Carry and roll with the different wedges.

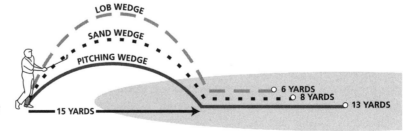

LOB WEDGE

SAND WEDGE

PITCHING WEDGE

6 YARDS
8 YARDS
13 YARDS

15 YARDS

accelerate the club through the shot. You may prefer to shorten your grip—choke down on the club—to give you more control on the shot.

Aim/Alignment

The process of aiming and aligning should begin from behind the ball. Visualize the shot, drawing an imaginary line back to your ball, and pick out an intermediate target on this line that is just in front of your ball. This is the spot at which you will aim the clubhead and align your body parallel left as you set up for the shot.

Set-Up

The set-up is similar to the set-up for a full shot with a couple of subtle changes. First, because the swing in shorter, the width of your stance will be a little narrower. The stance will also be slightly open. This means that your target foot is pulled back from the target line so that your feet, knees and hips are pointed slightly left of the target line. You will want to center the ball between your feet or position it just a little forward of center.

Stroke

The swing for a pitch shot is just a shorter (less backswing) version of the full swing. Start with a one-piece backswing emphasizing the arms and shoulder moving back as one and allowing the wrist to hinge naturally in the backswing (Figure 6.3) and the forwardswing. This swing should feel almost lazy. It should not be rushed on the backswing or the forwardswing, somewhat like the pendulum on a clock. Because a good sense of tempo and rhythm are so important for this type of shot, slow, smooth and easy would be a good swing thought. From the top of the backswing you want to feel your hands drop, allowing the weight of the clubhead to accelerate the club through the ball as your body turns toward your target and your weight shifts to your front foot. This should carry you to a nice shoulder-high finish. As in all short game shots, the length of the swing controls the length of the shot. The distance to the target and the club you have selected will determine the length of your backswing.

Fig. 6.3. Backswing for a pitch shot.

Fig. 6.4. *Illustration of the 7:30, 9:00 and 10:30 backswings to control the distance that shots carry with different clubs.*

7:30   **9:00**   **10:30**

Distance control on pitch shots requires a lot of experience and practice to become proficient. Dave Pelz (1999), a noted short game instructor, recommends a good drill to help you gain proficiency with pitch shots. Take your shag bag and set out targets about 10 yards apart, starting at 30 or 40 yards away. Hit several shots with each of your wedges (PW, SW and LW) making a backswing to 7:30, 9:00 and 10:30 on a clock face (Figure 6.4) for each of your wedges. Be sure to note how far the ball carries (not including the roll) with each wedge. Understanding how far the ball will carry with the three different swings will allow you to hit these shots with confidence on the course. Getting your pitch shots close will help to reduce the number of putts required, thus lowering your scores.

Chip Shots

Club Selection

For chip shots, the first thing you need to determine is which club to use. The best method to answer this question is to determine how far you want the ball to go in the air and how far you want it to roll on the green. You can select a club with as much loft as a sand wedge or as little loft as a 5- or 6-iron. Try to imagine where you want the ball to land on the green based on the slope of the green and how far the hole is cut from the edge of the green. This will determine how far the ball should carry in the air and how much you want it to roll. With a 6-iron, the ball will be carry only about 25% of the distance in the air and will roll the rest of the way to the hole. A sand wedge will carry the ball about 75% of the distance to the hole and have a much more limited amount of roll once it lands on the green (Figure 6.5).

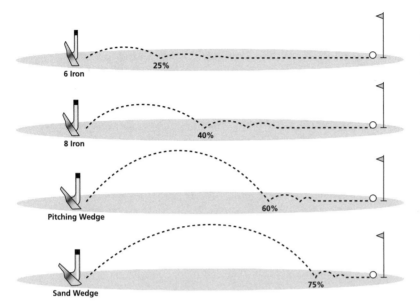

Fig. 6.5. Illustration of carry and roll for a chip shot with different clubs.

6 Iron — 25%

8 Iron — 40%

Pitching Wedge — 60%

Sand Wedge — 75%

A shot that is rolling on the green is the easiest type of shot to get close where distance and direction are important. Once a ball is lofted in the air it is hard to control or predict the reaction of the ball when it hits the green. Will the shot check up, will it release, will it get a bad bounce, etc? Try to make the choice of clubs and the shot as easy as possible by adhering to the old adage of "minimize air time and maximize ground time." In other words, use the least lofted club possible to land the ball 2 or 3 feet on the green and let it roll the rest of the way to the hole.

Because no two situations are the same—the lie, the slope of the green, the distance to the green, the distance to the hole and so forth all vary—avoid the pitfall of falling in love with using just one club for all of your chip shots around the green. A good way to learn which club will work best for you in different situations is to drop several balls just off of the practice green and chip a few balls with your sand wedge, pitching wedge, 8-iron and 6-iron. Make note of the different amounts of carry and roll that you get with each of the different clubs. This will help you to develop a feel for the carry to roll ratio that each club produces. This will also help you to develop confidence in chipping with more than just one club.

A variation on club selection for chip shots that has received a lot of attention in the last couple of years because of Tiger Woods is the use of a fairway wood. If you find your ball in long grass around the green you may want to try using a fairway wood. This club will slide through the grass with less resistance than an iron, which cuts through the grass. With less resistance, the fairway wood offers two advantages. First, the clubhead does not get twisted as much by the grass, keeping the shot on line better. Secondly, the clubhead does not decelerate as much, which affects the distance of the shot. Because some grass will be trapped between the ball and the clubface, and the fairway wood does not have a lot of loft, the shot will have less backspin and the ball will roll more than normal. The deeper the grass the more loft you will want on the fairway wood. Be sure to practice this shot before you try it on the course.

Aim/Alignment

Every shot in golf should begin from behind the ball. Visualize the shot, drawing an imaginary line back to your ball, and pick out an intermediate target on this line that is just in front of your ball. This is the spot at which you will aim the clubhead and then align your body parallel left of as you set up for the shot. Your feet, knees and hips should be aligned slightly open (left for RH golfers) to your actual target line.

Set-Up

The set-up for chipping requires a few adjustments from that of a full swing in order to make solid contact with the ball first and then the ground in a descending arc. You will want to use the same grip (overlapping, etc.) that you would use when making a shot with a full swing. However, you will want to choke down on the club so that the index finger of your right hand almost touches the shaft. This will bring you closer to the target line and give you more control of the swing. Because the stroke is relatively short you will want to narrow your stance, as you do when putting. The stroke is also more of a rocking motion, with the shoulders and arms like the stroke for putting and with very little lower body motion. Therefore, you want your feet and hips open, that is, your front foot is pulled back from the target line so that your feet and hips are angled left of the target line. This allows you to swing down the target line while limiting lower body motion. Once your feet are properly positioned, shift the majority (60–70 percent) of your weight to the front foot and leave it there throughout the entire swing. Again, you want very little lower body motion in the swing. Ball position and hand position are important in order to make a descending swing into the ball. The ball should be played rear of center, just inside your back foot. The hands should be moved closer to the target (ahead of the ball) at address so that the end of the grip is pointing toward your left hip (Figure 6.6).

You have made five distinct changes in the pre-swing fundamentals for a chip shot. You have:

1. shortened your grip (choked down on the club);
2. narrowed and opened your stance (feet and hips point left of the target line);
3. shifted 60–70 percent of your weight to your left foot;
4. positioned the ball back of the center of your stance toward your back foot; and
5. moved your hands forward so that the grip points toward your left hip.

Fig. 6.6. Set-up for a chip shot.

Stroke

The stroke for the chip shot is a mini-swing that begins by making a one-piece backswing, similar to putting. You will experience the most success and consistency if you keep your wrists firm, not allowing them to hinge on the backswing and for-wardswing. Using a one-piece swing thought, attempt to limit wrist action so that the swing triangle created at ad-dress remains intact during the swing, and let the club-head accelerate through the shot (Figure 6.7). Your weight should remain on your front foot and hands should remain closer to the target than the clubhead to ensure that you create a descending swing arc that allows the clubhead to contact the ball before the ground. Be-

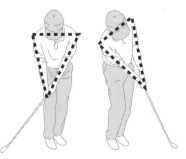

cause the swing for a chip shot is a little longer than that of a putt, the lower body will be more active. However, you want to limit this lower body motion to avoid hitting the shot off line. A drill that you may find beneficial for learning how far the ball will carry and roll is to imagine that you are tossing the ball with your hand, using an underhand toss-

Fig. 6.7. Backswing and follow through for a chip shot while maintaining the swing triangle.

ing motion, to the target. Focus on how long the arm swing should be in order to get the ball to go that given distance. Practice this by actually tossing a few balls to the hole in this manner. Then, using this thought as you are actually making the shot, "toss" the ball with the clubhead to the target.

Putting

Putting is arguably the most important stroke in the game of golf. If you look at any scorecard you will see that 50 percent of the strokes that constitute par are putts. Dave Pelz found through studying scores over several years that on average, just over 40 percent of the shots in a round of golf are putts. Harvey Penick (1992) liked to say, "A good putter is a match for anyone. A bad putter is a match for no one." Unfortunately, most players neglect to practice putting as much as they practice their full swing. At best, they will half-heartedly go through the motions of practicing around the green a few minutes before teeing off on the first hole. While some golfers like to use lack of time as an excuse for not practicing putting, most golfers view practice on the putting green as boring and monotonous. To reduce boredom and make practice more beneficial, invent fun games to play on the practice green, either alone or with friends. By making practice fun you will be more willing to do it on a regular basis. If you seriously want to lower your scores, spend at least 50 percent of your practice time on your short game (Tiger Woods spends up to 70 percent of his time on the short game).

Grip

Establishing correct hand placement on your putter is easier than determining how to put your hands on the club for the full swing. The grip on most putters has flat sides and a flat surface on the top to facilitate the positioning of the thumbs. Simply start with both palms facing each other (almost like saying a prayer over that 3-foot putt) so that the thumbs of both hands extend directly down the midline of the grip. Like gripping the club for a full swing, you will want to join or link your hands together. You may prefer to use the same type of grip (interlocking, overlapping or ten-finger) that you use when making a full swing. This is not a bad idea if you are just taking up the game since it gives a feeling of consistency and perhaps some confidence in your hold on the club.

However, the most commonly used method for joining your hands together when putting is the reverse overlapping grip. The reverse overlapping grip places all of the fingers of the right hand on the club. The index finger of the left hand then overlaps one to three fingers of the right hand, depending on personal preference (Figure 6.8). Another idea that you may find helpful is to extend the index finger of your right hand down the grip. Pointing the right index finger down the grip is helpful in maintaining firm wrists so that the left wrist does not break, down knocking the putt off line. It also serves as a pointer, helping to show the way to the hole.

Another difference in the way you hold the putter involves grip pressure. Since golf is a game of feel, particularly in the short game, light grip pressure is essential. Holding the club lightly allows for more tactile feedback through your hands and fingers relative to the length and speed of the swing as the putter swings back and through the ball. Light grip pressure also gives you a good feel for contact with the ball. It is important that your grip pressure remains constant throughout the swing. Tightening your grip pressure, particularly in the forwardswing, produces a jerky decelerating stoke that will alter the distance and direction of the putt. It is the combination of tactile feedback (that you get through your hands) and visual feedback (from the result of the putt) that helps you to learn to adjust the length and speed of the swing in order to get the ball to consistently roll the correct distance.

In the search for a putting stroke that will hold up under pressure, golfers will often experiment with a new type of grip. One of the most popular grip changes in recent years has been the cross-handed or left-hand low grip (Figure 6.9). This type of grip is seen regularly on the professional tours and even among average golfers. Having the left hand lower than the right helps to keep the wrists firm and avoid the left wrist breaking down or hinging in the swing. Dave Pelz (2003) found through studies of various putting styles that the left-hand low is the second

Fig. 6.8. Reverse overlapping grip for putting.

Fig. 6.9. Left-hand low grip for putting.

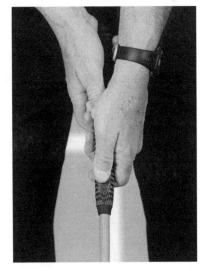

Fig. 6.10. Claw grip.

most accurate method of putting. Another, more radical grip change that some golfers have tried is the claw grip (Figure 6.10).

Aim/Alignment

Aiming the clubhead and aligning your body correctly to the target line is important for every shot, especially when you are putting. To begin the aim/alignment process, position yourself several feet behind the ball so that the ball is between you and the hole. Bend down as close to the surface of the green as you can. This allows you to see the contours of the green better. Now look toward the hole and visualize a line from the hole to your ball. If the green is level between your ball and the hole you can simply aim (square) the face of the putter to that line. However, if the green has a slope that will cause the putt to break (roll) either left or right, try to visualize the line of the curve your ball will take as it rolls to the hole (Figure 6.11). One of the simplest and most effective methods of "seeing" this line is to imagine tossing a bucket of water across the green and visualizing the path the water will take as it runs toward the hole. As you "see" the water curving toward the hole, try to pick a spot on the green at the apex of this curve. This is the spot at which you will aim the face of the putter. Then align your feet, knees, hips, shoulders and eyes parallel to this target line (Figure 6.12). When you recheck your aim and alignment, rotate your head and eyes down the target line rather than lifting and turning your head to look at the hole.

Fig. 6.11 (left). Lining up a breaking putt. Imagine the line the ball will take as it rolls to the hole. Take into account the speed of the green, the slope of the green, and the length of the putt. Putt to the apex of the break and let gravity do its job.

Fig. 6.12. (right). Set-up for a putt.

Set-Up

When you are setting up over a putt, it is important to feel relaxed and comfortable. If you watch golfers as they are putting, you will see a wide variety of set-ups; however, certain characteristics are common to them all (Figure 6.12).

1. The putter is soled flat on the ground.

2. The feet are spread a comfortable distance apart for good balance.

3. The body bends forward from the hips with the arms hanging straight down from the shoulders.

4. The eyes are directly over the ball and the target line.

5. The ball is played somewhere between the center of the stance and the inside of the right foot.

Stroke

The putting stroke is a smooth pendular motion that should involve only a rocking motion of the shoulders and arms back and through with no lower body movement and no bending of the wrists. The two main factors involved in putting are distance and direction. Of these two, distance—the length of the putt—is the most important. Although learning to control the direction of the putt is almost instinctive, learning to consistently control the distance the ball will roll requires much practice on a regular basis. If your first putt is too long or short, it will leave you with a long difficult second putt—which is the main cause of most three-putt greens.

Three factors that will influence the distance the ball rolls are the length of the swing, the pace of the swing and contact with the sweet spot of the clubface. Your putter has a sweet spot that is normally marked in some manner, usually a painted line(s) near the center of the clubhead. In order to develop consistency in the distance and direction of your putts, you must learn to make contact with the ball in the sweet spot of the putter. Even if your putter is moving down the desired line but you contact the ball toward the toe or heel side of the sweet spot, the clubhead will twist slightly, creating side spin and causing the ball to roll away from the hole. You will also lose distance on a putt that is struck off-center. A putt that is intended to roll 20 feet may only roll

15–16 feet if struck off-center. The farther you miss the sweet spot the more the direction and distance of the putt will be affected.

If changing your grip (see above) does not provide the improvement in your putting that you are looking for, you may want to consider experimenting with altering your style of putting (the method that you use to swing the putter). Sam Snead, winner of more (84) PGA tournaments, than any other golfer, began to suffer from "the yips" (the inability to make a smooth putting stroke when under pressure) late in his career. In order to overcome the yips he started putting croquet style, facing the hole with the ball between his feet. This style of putting was soon deemed illegal by the USGA (you cannot stand astride your line of putt). In response, Snead switched to putting sidesaddle (standing beside the target line).

Several years ago the long putter was introduced, however, only a small minority of golfers uses one. The long putter is anchored against the chest with the left hand and the club is swung with just your right hand (Figure 6.13). Those who have problems with back pain while putting might benefit most from this putting style because the more upright

*Fig. 6.13 (left).
Putting with a long
putter.*

*Fig. 6.14 (right).
Putting with a belly
putter.*

stance employed with the long putter helps take stress off of the lower back. A more recent style of putting that has been more widely accepted is the use of the "belly" putter. Like the long putter, the belly putter is anchored against the body (the stomach or lower torso), but you hold and swing the club with both hands in a more conventional manner (Figure 6.14). Both the long and the belly putters, which are anchored against the body, make it easier to keep the club swinging along the intended target line. Dave Pelz's (2003) studies on putting indicate that the belly putting style is the most accurate method of putting.

Distance

The amount of force needed to roll the ball the correct distance comes from the shoulders and arms, which form the swing triangle. As a beginner, you will probably have more success with a one-piece (one lever), pendular stroke. This one-piece stroke is similar to the motion of the pendulum of a grandfather clock. The shoulders and arms swing the putter away from, and back through, the ball with no movement in the wrist. Smooth acceleration is important for obtaining accurate distance on a putt. There should be no noticeable change in the speed of the stroke from the backswing to the forwardswing. If the clubhead is accelerated too quickly into the ball, or decelerated as it approaches the ball, you will have difficulty with distance control on your putts.

The length of the backswing plays an important role in the speed of the stroke on the forwardswing. If the backswing is too long, the tendency is to instinctively decelerate the clubhead as it approaches the ball. Focus instead on making a shorter backswing and a longer follow-through. The follow-through should actually be a little longer than the backswing. When you are just beginning to learn how to putt, try setting your putter down and just rolling the ball across the green toward the hole with your hand, using an underhand motion. After you develop a good feel for rolling the ball the correct the distance with your hand, practice with your putter using this same image of rolling the ball across the green with your hand. This will help you to develop a good feel for the swinging motion of the arms—as opposed to a hitting motion—and the length and speed of the swing. Once you have developed a good feel for putting the ball the correct distance on a flat surface you will want to practice on a green that has a slope so that you can learn how to adjust the length of your swing when putting uphill or downhill.

Direction

The direction you must stroke the ball is instinctive or intuitive. After squaring the club face to the target line and getting into your set-up position, keeping the club face square to the target line is simply a matter of maintaining the swing triangle throughout the stroke and keeping your left wrist firm. If the left wrist breaks, the clubface will turn away from the target, resulting in putts that roll left of the hole. The slope of the green will also affect the direction the ball rolls. The amount of slope and the speed of the putt will both factor into how far the putt will break. Through experience, gained from practicing and playing, you will learn to judge how much a putt will break as it follows the slope of the green.

Concentration

Golfers who struggle on the putting green often find that their difficulty results from poor fundamentals, a lack of concentration and/or a lack of confidence. A lack of confidence will cause unnecessary stress and tension, which negatively affects your stroke mechanics and concentration. You must remain focused on the length and pace of the swing until the ball is well on its way to the hole. The desire to see the ball as it rolls toward the hole will alter your focus causing a breakdown in your swing mechanics. If you "peek" too soon, the resulting movement of the head, body and/or eyes will alter the swing path, swing pace and contact with the sweet spot. All of these factors have a negative effect on the putt's distance and direction. In order to avoid taking 3, 4 or even 5 putts per hole, it is essential to train yourself to maintain your concentration.

Fig. 6.15. Listen, don't look, for the ball to drop in the hole.

Your head and eyes should remain motionless over the ball until the ball is well on its way to the hole. One method of maintaining your concentration longer is to train yourself when practicing to keep your eyes focused on the spot on the green where the ball was (Figure 6.15) and *listen* for the ball to drop in the cup rather than *looking* to see if it goes in the hole.

7 Errors: Identification and Correction

Golf is a game of misses. How many times in any given round do you hit a shot that is perfect? The average golfer will hit 5 or fewer shots in a round of golf that could be considered perfect or near perfect. The remaining 80 plus shots were not what was desired. If this is true, why do millions of golfers continue to return to the golf course to repeat the same error over and over? Coop (1993) suggests that since golf offers intermittent reinforcement, golfers stay with the game because "…psychological research has found that behaviors that are acquired on the basis of intermittent reinforcement are the behaviors most resistant to extinction" (p. 7). Trying to implement change is very difficult because change feels different and uncomfortable, and satisfactory results take much time and practice.

Even without considerable time spent on the practice range, your memory of those few good shots that you hit with the old swing will still linger. But when you find yourself in a situation where a good shot under pressure is required and you have not established a good mental blueprint of your new swing and swing thoughts (developed through practice) you tend to revert to the "old method" of executing your swing. Your mental comfort zone reverts when under stress. Due to the practice time required to execute change, many golfers instead elect to accept swing deficiencies or faults as a normal part of their game. However, if you are willing to endure the frustrations of getting used to the feel of a new swing and the initial poor results which may ensue, and you can stay focused on having a more consistent, repeatable swing, it is possible to correct the errors in your swing.

The cause of swing errors can be separated into three distinct categories:

1. Mistakes in **pre-swing fundamentals** – those that occur as you prepare to execute the shot including improper grip, alignment and set-up.
2. Mistakes in **course management** – those that occur during the decision-making process prior to making a shot. Those mistakes include miscalculating club selection, type of lie, the effect of weather conditions, ability level, etc.
3. **Swing errors** – those that occur during the actual swing itself.

Toski et al. (1984) state that the first two categories are cognitive mistakes (those made in the "thinking" process), and they account for 90 percent of the errors in a golf shot. The remaining 10 percent of mistakes fall in the third category, swing errors (physical mistakes). This idea that most mistakes related to golf are mental rather than physical is generally shared by those in the golf teaching profession. What should be of paramount importance to you is that this is an area in which you can make real improvements in your game. By practicing your pre-swing fundamentals and reading about and practicing course management skills (see chapter 10 and the references) you can begin to eliminate the major portion—the mental area—of your mistakes. The physical portion of your mistakes—those swing errors—can be reduced by work at the practice range attempting to build a sound fundamental swing that is repeatable, even under the pressures of competition.

Before time can productively be spent on solving swing errors, you must first have at least a basic understanding of the ball flight laws. As mentioned earlier, the trajectory of your shot consists of two component—direction and distance. Applying your understanding of the ball flight laws can enable you to better understand your swing errors and how to make corrections. The *PGA Teaching Manual* (1990) defines ball flight laws as "the physical forces which are absolutes in influencing the flight of the ball" (p. 47). When examined at impact with the ball, those forces, or laws, are listed and defined below.

Ball Flight Laws

1. **Clubhead speed** – the speed at which the clubhead is moving through impact is the primary determinant of the distance a ball will fly. Some of the factors that affect clubhead speed include: the physical characteristics of the club (length, weight, shaft flex, etc.), the arc of the swing, and the height of the player.
2. **Path of the clubhead** – the direction in which the club on a full swing is traveling at impact in relation to the target line determines the initial direction a ball will travel.
3. **Squareness (centeredness) of contact** – making contact squarely in the "sweet spot" of the club has a direct relationship to both the direction and the distance the ball will travel.
4. **Clubface position** – the clubface position at impact is a strong determinant in the final direction a ball will travel. If the club-

face is open or closed at impact, a clockwise (CW) or counter-clockwise (CCW) side-spin is placed on the ball, which will cause the ball to curve right or left.

5. **Angle of attack** – at impact, the angle at which the club is either descending or ascending is a contributor to both the distance a ball will fly and its trajectory.

Also, the position on the ball that your club strikes will affect distance and trajectory. A ball struck on its top half will fly downward into the ground. If struck at its equator the ball will fly relatively low, and if it's struck below the equator it will fly relatively high.

In attempting to correct mistakes that lead to errors in your golf shots, using your knowledge of the ball flight laws is helpful in enabling you to analyze your shot pattern and to make the necessary adjustment(s) to correct the problem. If this proves unsuccessful, try to avoid all the well-meaning advice from friends and instead visit a club professional or your local teacher for a lesson.

Shots That Go Right and Left

Directional problems are sure to plague you at some point in your golfing experience. Because the trajectory of the ball must conform to the ball flight laws, when your ball flies in any direction other than a straight line to the target, it is because the law of swing path, of club-face position, or both, were violated. There are nine possible directions that the ball can take while in flight (Figure 7.1).

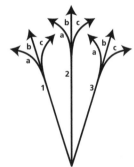

1. *Swing Path across the intended target line* (outside to inside)
   a. Clubface closed to the swing path (**snap** or **duck hook**)
   b. Clubface square to the swing path (**pull**)
   c. Clubface open to the swing path (**pull slice**)

2. *Swing Path straight down the intended target line*
   a. Clubface closed to the swing path (**hook**)
   b. Clubface square to the swing path (**straight shot**)
   c. Clubface open to the swing path (**slice**)

3. *Swing Path across the intended target line* (inside to outside)
   a. Clubface closed to the swing path (**hook**)
   b. Clubface square to the swing path (**push**)
   c. Clubface open to the swing path (**slice**)

Fig. 7.1. Ball flight patterns.

The direction that the ball flies is affected principally by the direction of your swing path. There are three swing paths—down the intended line, outside-inside, and inside-out (Figure 7.1). The clubface will impart side-spin if it faces left or right of your swing path, causing the ball to curve left or right. There are three clubface positions—closed, square, and open (Figure 7.1). While the side spin created by the clubface position causes the shot to curve, it does not influence the direction of the shot as much as the swing path.

Shots That Go Right

(*The following instructions for correcting directional errors are for right-handed golfers. Left-handed golfers can merely mirror-reverse these instructions.*)

Fig. 7.2 (top). Push occurs when the swing path comes inside-out across the target line and the clubface is square to the swing path.

Fig. 7.3 (bottom). Slice caused by opening the clubface to the target line. Ball starts straight then curves right.

1. **Push** – a shot that moves in a straight line to the right of your target (Figure 7.2)
2. **Slice** – a shot that starts out straight (Figure 7.3) or to the left (Figure 7.4) of your target, but with CW side-spin, curves to the right and finishes to the right of your target.
3. **Fade** – a shot that starts to the left of the target, and curves back toward the target, finishing very close to the original target line (Figure 8.1).

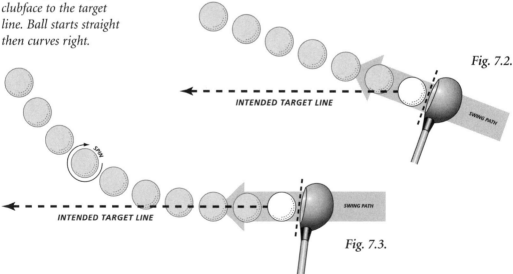

INTENDED TARGET LINE

SWING PATH

Fig. 7.2.

SPIN

INTENDED TARGET LINE

SWING PATH

Fig. 7.3.

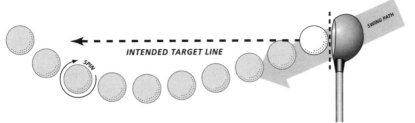

Fig. 7.4. Slice starting to the left of the target, then curving right due to side-spin imparted at impact.

Push Corrections

A push (inside to outside swing path with clubface square to path) generally is caused by improper alignment, a swing plane that is too flat, or having the ball too far back in your stance. Poor alignment is the first place to look. This problem plagues even highly skilled golfers. If you are constantly making this error, use some extra clubs to form an 'H' while at the practice tee to help get properly aligned during your pre-shot routine and as you set up to the ball (Figure 3.12). If your alignment is correct, have a professional or knowledgeable friend check your swing plane. If your swing plane is too flat it will cause you to block out the shot with your hips, sending it to the right of your target. Finally, pay attention to the position of the ball in your stance. As a part of your pre-shot routine, practice positioning the ball correctly in your stance to avoid directional errors.

Slice Corrections

By far the most common and perplexing directional error is the slice (outside to inside swing path with clubface square to intended target). Just as for every quick weight-loss gimmick on the market, there is at least one suggestion from people you encounter on the golf course, or revolutionary new idea from some equipment manufacturer, to prevent or reduce slicing.

When your shots are slicing, the first place to look is your alignment. Get a friend to help you check to see that your feet, hips, shoulders and head (eyes) are all aligned squarely to the intended line of flight. Because a majority of directional errors are a result of alignment problems, this is the best place to begin your search for a solution. Improper alignment often causes a swing path that comes from outside-inside, and a clubface which remains square to the intended line of flight.

If your alignment is correct and your swing path continues to come from outside-inside, across the intended swing path, the culprit is commonly a swing that is not properly sequenced. When your swing is properly sequenced, the downswing is initiated from the ground up with the lower body rather than the upper body. The target heel replants into its original set-up position, and the knees and hips move laterally, with the hips turning toward the target. Your swing triangle should remain intact as the large muscles of the back and shoulders begin to turn toward your target, with your dominant elbow remaining close to your side. The hands and wrists should remain in a fully cocked position until they drop between shoulder and waist level where centrifugal force causes them to unhinge, thus allowing the clubface to square-up naturally at impact. This sequence, if begun from a proper position at the top of the backswing, will bring the club back to the ball from just slightly inside the target line.

When the downswing is initiated from the top of the backswing by an improper dominant shoulder rotation, the resulting swing path finds the clubhead outside of the target line prior to impact. To correct this problem, focus on making a one-piece takeaway with the large muscles of the back and shoulders and then making a smooth transition into the downswing, starting from the ground up rather than spinning out with

the shoulders. Avoid trying to "hit" the ball too hard, which tends to cause the dominant shoulder to move outside of the preferred swing plane instead of correctly moving under the chin. This swing error often results in an incorrect weight shift, an incomplete finish position, and a weak, ineffectual slice. Premature uncocking of your wrists at the beginning of the downswing ("casting" the clubhead) will also throw the clubhead outside of the intended swing path (Figure 7.5). In addition, casting the club will cause a se-

Fig. 7.5. "Casting" the club. The wrists are uncocked at the beginning of the downswing.

vere loss of clubhead speed and a resulting loss of distance. Attempt to delay the uncocking of your wrists until your hands reach almost waist level in the downswing.

If your shot starts out down the intended line of flight but slices (Figure 7.3), the culprit is an open clubface at impact. Because the release of your hands as they near waist level happens in just a fraction of a second, you cannot consciously square the clubface at impact. Instead, you have to just "let it happen." If the clubface is not squaring naturally, try reducing your grip tension and the tension in your arms and shoulders. Too much tension will slow the release of your hands and prevent your forearms from rotating freely. Tension will also inhibit your ability to feel the club as it swings.

The position of your hands as you grip the club must also be taken into account. If one or both of your hands are in a weak position (Figure 7.6), this may prevent you from squaring the clubface. To strengthen your grip, rotate your target hand slightly so that you can see two or three knuckles on the back of your hand. Also, check to see that the palm of your dominant hand is facing your target and that the V formed by the thumb and index finger of that hand is pointing between the ear and shoulder on the dominant side of your body. Remember, your grip is your only connection with the club; therefore, proper tension and hand positioning are important to ensure that the hands and club interact properly during the swing.

Another potential cure for a slice that results from an open clubface is to practice your backswing by making a one-piece takeaway for the first 18 inches or so, rather than fanning the toe of the club open at the start of the backswing. When your golf club reaches a position parallel to the ground in the backswing, the clubface—more specifically the scoring lines on the clubface—should be at right angles or perpendicular to the ground or even slightly hooded towards the ground—as opposed to facing the sky (Figure 4.4). This will help to get the hands in the proper position at the top of the swing, with the thumbs under the shaft and pointed at your target with the target wrist relatively flat—as determined by your grip at address (Figure 7.7).

As you practice these techniques to try to "cure" your slice, have someone who is knowledgeable about golf swings watch you to ensure that you are actually doing what you think you are doing. Many times what you think you are doing related to your swing is in reality something completely different. If you are not employing a new technique correctly, not only will you fail to get the desired results, you will just begin to ingrain another poor swing

Fig. 7.6. Weak grip.

Fig. 7.7. Correct grip.

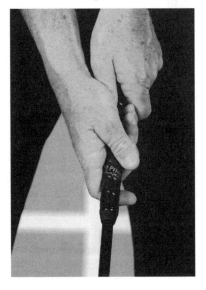

habit into the mental blueprint you have of that skill, thereby complicating the process.

Fade

A fade is not normally considered to be a directional error, instead it is a shot that better golfers use if their natural swings favors curving the ball from left to right. They can also use a fade to get out of a bad lie (Chapter 8, Figure 8.1). Jack Nicklaus and Tiger Woods are two of the most successful professionals of our time at employing a fade as a natural shot. A fade offers the advantage of a predictable ball flight and the ability to make the ball sit more softly on the green. Lee Trevino, a very successful "left-to-right player of the ball" says that "you can talk to a fade, but a draw will not listen." By following your natural swing pattern and allowing the ball to naturally curve back toward your target, you will generally know where to expect your ball to end up and you can use this knowledge to avoid trouble, e.g., trees, water, etc.

Shots That Go Left

1. **Pull** – a shot that flies in a straight line to the left of the target (Figure 7.8).
2. **Hook** – a shot that starts out straight or to the right of the target, but with CCW side-spin curves left, finishing to the left of the target (Figure 7.9).
3. **Draw** – a shot that starts to the right of the target, and curves back toward the target, finishing very close to the original target line (Figure 8.1).

Fig. 7.8. Pull occurs when the swing path comes outside-in across the intended target line and the club face remains square to the swing path.

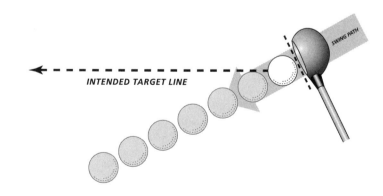

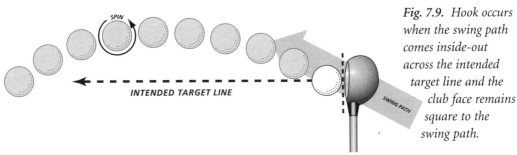

Fig. 7.9. Hook occurs when the swing path comes inside-out across the intended target line and the club face remains square to the swing path.

Pull Corrections

A pull (outside-inside swing path with clubface square to the swing path, Figure 7.8) is generally caused by improper alignment, a swing plane that is too upright, or having the ball too far forward in your stance. If your alignment is correct, the problem may be related to your swing plane. When your swing plane is too upright it allows your dominant shoulder to move outside of your target shoulder, which brings the club across the swing path from the outside. Ball position is the last place to check if you are still hitting shots that go straight to the left of your intended target.

Hook Corrections

The hook, like the slice, has two basic shapes and can be corrected in essentially the same way that you would correct a slice. If your shots are starting out away from your intended target line and then hooking back toward it (Figure 7.9), you may be starting your downswing too far inside the intended line with the clubface square to your target, or you may be misaligned in your set-up. In the majority of cases, a hook of this type can be cured by ensuring that your body position (feet, hips and shoulders) is correct.

A shot that starts out on the intended line, or just slightly outside it, and hooks back beyond the target line (Figure 7.10) is the result of a

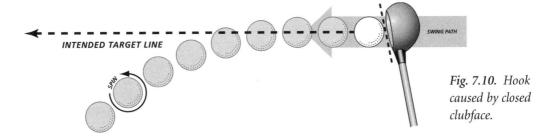

Fig. 7.10. Hook caused by closed clubface.

closed clubface. This may be caused either by a faulty grip or by an improper hand position at the top of your backswing. Should either or both of your hands—most commonly the target hand—be turned too far away from the target (too strong) at address, and you make a normal full rotation of the hands and forearms in the downswing, the clubface will end up in a position that is closed to the intended target line at impact. By keeping the V's of both hands between the dominant side ear and shoulder, this can be avoided. Like the slice, a hook is many times the result of improper hand position at the top of the backswing. Make some swings, stopping at the top to check the position of your target wrist. If that wrist is not relatively flat, you will have difficulty in consistently getting the clubface back to square at impact.

Draw

Like a fade, a draw (Figure 8.1) is not normally considered a directional error, instead it is a shot that better golfers use if their natural swing favors curving the ball from right to left, or if they are trying to get out of a bad lie. A draw does offer the advantage of distance over shots that curve to the right since the ball will get more roll after it hits the ground. If your natural swing favors a shot that curves from right to left, use it for getting more distance, and be confidant that you know the shape of the shot and where it will end up.

Some checkpoints to work on to correct shots that go from right to left include:

1. **Alignment** – Stand behind the ball and line it up with your intended target by visualizing the target line discussed in pre-swing fundamentals (see Chapter 3). Then set your feet, hips, shoulders and head (eyes) on a line parallel to your intended target line.

2. **Grip** – As you take your hold on the club, align the V's of your target and dominant hands to a point between your ear and shoulder on the dominant side of your body (Figure 3.8). Then, relax your grip so that the club is held securely, but so that there is no tension in the hands, arms and shoulders.

3. **Hand position** – The position of your hands at the top of your backswing, especially your target hand, will play a big role in whether you are able to square the clubface at contact. Check to see that your target wrist is relatively flat (a fairly straight line is

formed by your forearm and the back of your hand) at the top of your backswing (Figure 7.7).

4. **Swing plane** – Your hands should be almost directly over your dominant shoulder at the top of your swing if your swing plane is correct (Figure 7.7).

5. **Swing, do not "hit"** – Your swing should be a large-muscle motion. Avoid allowing the hands and the arms to initiate or lead into the downswing. It should be a case of the dog (big muscles) wagging the tail (the hands), not the reverse.

Mishit Shots

Topping

There is nothing quite as discouraging as seeing your ball skidding and bouncing along the fairway rather than rising up into the air and sailing toward your target. This type of skidding, bouncing shot—called topping—occurs when the club contacts the top half of the ball after the clubhead has passed the bottom of its arc and is on the way up towards the finish of the swing (Figure 7.11). Topping results from violating the ball flight law—angle of attack—which dictates that, with the irons, the ball should be struck below its equator with a descending blow just before the

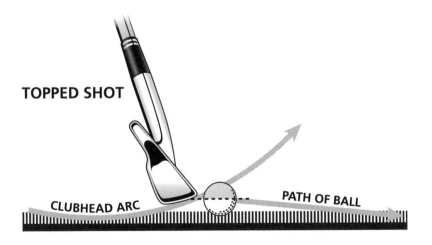

Fig. 7.11. Topped shot.

TOPPED SHOT

CLUBHEAD ARC   **PATH OF BALL**

clubhead reaches the bottom of its arc. When this is done correctly, you will see your divot appear just in front of where the ball was sitting at address, and your ball will rise effortlessly into the air on its way to your target. There are several potential causes for topping, including excess tension, trying to "pick the ball up," changing the swing lever length during the swing, excess lateral motion during the swing (not staying within your foundation created at address), or trying to swing too hard.

Tension, either from a fear of failure or from simply gripping the club too tightly, will cause a poorly timed swing that has excessive head and body motion or a poor release of the hands. Tension from a fear of failure will also cause you to shift your focus from the ball to the target before you actually strike the ball. By developing a positive mental image of the shot in your pre-shot routine, and by relaxing the tension in your hands, arms and upper body as you set up for the shot, you can help to cure this problem.

The attempt to "pick the ball up" that often results in a topped shot becomes a self-perpetuating effort in futility which causes two problems. First, the length of your swing lever established at address shortens (flexes)—perhaps from too much effort—resulting in a decreased radius or swing arc and an altered angle of approach. Secondly, trying to pick the ball up combined with trying to swing too hard results in a poor weight shift; you are staying back on your dominant side. To overcome these two problems, work on developing a tempo with your swing triangle that is the same regardless of the distance. If you need more distance, use a longer club, not a faster swing.

Fat Shot

A fat shot occurs when your clubhead contacts the ground before it contacts the ball, dissipating the energy into the ground instead of the golf ball (Figure 7.12). The result is a shot that does not travel as far as you had intended, and in some cases goes only a few feet. Like the topped shot, many fat shots are the result of a poor weight shift and of trying to swing the club too hard. Other causes of a fat shot include collapsing the dominant side and a premature uncocking of the wrists during the downswing. The cures for the fat shot are very similar to those for a topped shot and include:

1. Having a positive mental image of the shot, a comfortable, relaxed set-up, and a smooth swing tempo;

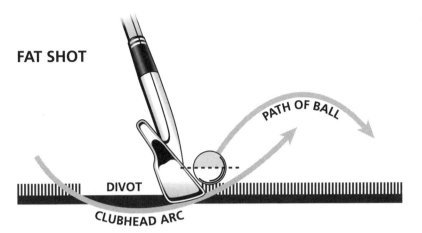

FAT SHOT

Fig. 7.12. Fat shot.

2. Not letting the dominant side collapse so that the dominant shoulder dips, which keeps your weight on that side. Keeping the weight there too long allows the clubhead to get ahead of your hands, causing the club to contact the ground behind the ball; and

3. Avoiding being "handsy" during your swing: Let the pace of the swing be controlled by the large muscles of the back and shoulders rather than by the hands.

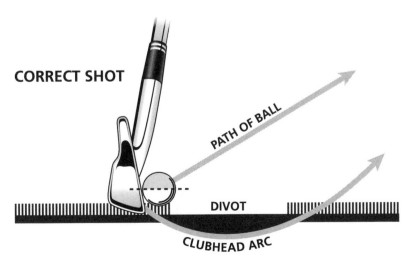

CORRECT SHOT

Fig. 7.13. Correct shot.

Shanking

The most feared word among high handicappers and many low hand-icappers is "shank." A shank is a shot in which the ball is contacted by the hosel of the club first and will usually fly off at a 45° to 90° angle to the intended line of flight. Many a ball has been lost or deposited into a yard, parking lot, or hazard this way. A shank is caused when the club approaches the ball from outside your intended swing path. The most unfortunate thing about this type of shot is that it is often followed by many more until you seek help from a pro, or take a short vacation from golf. The most fortunate thing about a shank is that it is relatively easy to cure. Some common causes of shanking and their cures are:

1. **Starting the club outside of the target line on the back swing** – Check to be sure that as you start the club back, it moves along your intended line, or just inside that line.

2. **Grabbing or regripping the club** – If you have allowed the heel of your target hand to lose contact with the grip at the top of your backswing (Figure 7.14), you will instinctively grab or re-grip the club as you start your downswing. This throws the club-head outside the intended line. As you set up to the ball, keep your grip tension light, and allow the large muscles to control your backswing.

3. **Casting the club on the downswing** – This occurs in trying to hit the ball too hard, when the dominant hand takes over at the start of the downswing. Loosen your grip and try to think "swing" rather than "hit" as you begin the downswing. Tempo, or the pace of your swing, is a key ingredient at this time.

4. **Excess body sway on short game shots when you are executing a less than full swing** – Swaying may be caused by a lack of focus, or even over-confidence. You are moving outside of the founda-tion you created during the pre-shot routine and your head then becomes positioned ahead of the ball.

This chapter has presented a number of commonly found golfing faults. When a fault (or faults) are identified in your game, you are faced with options. It is the authors' position that you should then become very familiar with a practice range. The mantra bears repeating: to at-tain the next level requires sound practice (see Chapter 9).

Fig. 7.14. Loss of contact at the top of the backswing.

8 Trouble Shots

Golf courses are laid out amongst some of the most wonderful, scenic terrain that nature has to offer. Enjoying a walk over the hills, beside the streams and the beautiful landscaping surrounding the golf course is a big part of the attraction of the game for many golfers. At times, the uneven terrain and landscaping, along with obstacles such as sand and water that are added by the course architect present obstacles that necessitate "trouble" shots that test your creativity and your golf skills. If viewed in a positive manner, as a challenge to your skills rather than as a threat, these trouble shots will actually add to your enjoyment of the game.

This chapter will help to you to lower your scores by providing you with the information necessary to successfully execute shots where the ball is not sitting on a tee or on a perfectly flat, manicured fairway. By using this information along with your knowledge of the ball flight laws (see Chapter 7) and your creativity, you will learn to hit shots from sidehill lies; shots that must go left, right, high, or low; shots when the weather intervenes; shots from the rough and the sand; and even shots where you must make an unorthodox swing to advance the ball. Learning how to adjust your set-up and swing for these different shots will help you to feel more confident when faced with an unfriendly lie and will enable you to enjoy the challenge of the game more. It is important to remember that getting your ball on the green is not always possible when faced with a trouble shot. Quite often the objective will be simply to get your ball out of the trouble situation, even if you must hit the ball back in the direction of the tee. In these situations, the trouble shot was a success if your next shot is from the fairway with a clear shot to the green.

Intentional Draw and Fade

Sometimes you will find it necessary to hit shots that must curve left or right because your target line is obstructed by trees or other obsta-

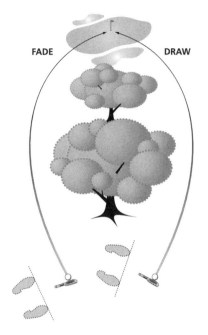

Fig. 8.1. Draw and fade.

cles, or when there is a big bend (dog leg) in the fairway. An intentional draw (a shot that curves from right to left for RH golfers) or fade (a shot that curves from left to right for RH golfers) (Figure 8.1) are both executed in basically the same manner. First, align your feet, hips and shoulders on a parallel line away from the trouble (the direction that you want the shot to start). Next, aim the clubface at your intended target (the direction that you want the shot to finish). When adjusting the aim of the clubface, be sure to aim the clubface and then take your grip. Otherwise, at contact with the ball, the clubface will be square to your swing path and the shot will not curve back toward your target.

After you complete your set-up for an intentional draw or fade, simply swing down the target line that is formed by your feet, hips and shoulders. The shot will start out down the target line that you established at address and begin to curve back toward your target (the direction that you aimed the club face). As you are preparing to hit this type of shot, consider the loft of the club that you want to use for the shot. As the loft of the clubface increases you get more backspin and less sidespin. Therefore, it will be more difficult to make shots curve left or right with more lofted clubs like your 9-iron and your wedges. Once you have selected a club and gone through your pre-shot routine, key on maintaining your tempo, swing triangle and concentration. Doubts about your abilities, or the outcome of the shot, will lead to peeking too soon to see where the ball is going, thus ruining the shot. Stay focused and trust that the laws of physics will cause the ball to curve in the desired direction. Practice this type of shot before you try it on the course so that you will have confidence in your abilities and the outcome.

High and Low Shots

Sometimes you may not be able to curve the shot around an obstruction, instead you must hit over or under the obstruction. Like an intentional draw or fade, high and low shots can be executed quite successfully by following a few simple guidelines when setting up for the shot—with a little practice.

Altering the trajectory of a shot involves a combination of club selection and ball position. Moving the ball toward your front foot increases the loft of the club and the trajectory of the shot, while moving the ball toward your back foot will produce the opposite result. Because the loft of the club is altered as the ball position changes it is difficult to predict the trajectory of the shot unless you have practiced these shots before attempting them on the course. When choosing a club, check to be sure the club has the correct loft so that there is no doubt that the shot will either easily clear the obstruction or stay under the obstruction. You do not want to have to play your next shot from a similar, or even a worse lie.

When setting up for a high shot, play the ball more forward in your stance, and place slightly more weight on your back foot (Figure 8.2). For a low shot, begin by playing the ball back in your stance and placing slightly more weight on your front foot. Also, move your hands forward, similar to a chip shot (Figure 8.3), and make a shorter backswing. Then, simply focus on making a good shoulder turn and on accelerating smoothly in the forward swing so that you do not alter your timing and spoil the shot. Because of the altered trajectory of high and low shots, the total distance of each of these shots will be less than that of a normal shot. Therefore, when choosing a landing area you may need to settle for a landing area in a wide part of the fairway in front of the green, rather than on the green itself. In situations like this it is helpful to remember that getting out of trouble and safely back in play is the main objective.

Uneven Lies

Because golf courses follow the natural slope of the terrain, finding your ball on the side of a hill or knoll is quite common. The difficulty of hitting from an uneven lie can be overcome by adjusting your club selection, aim/alignment, ball position and body weight to overcome the effects

Fig. 8.2 (top). Set-up for a high shot.
Fig. 8.3 (bottom). Set-up for a low shot.

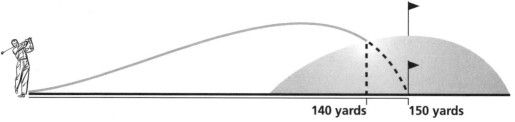

140 yards   **150 yards**

Fig. 8.4. Illustration of how elevation affects the distance that your shot will carry.

of the slope. Because all shots from an uneven lie tend to curve left or right, a good starting point is to group the uneven lies into two groups—up and down. Shots in the "up" group, where the shot is either being hit uphill or the where the ball is up above your feet will curve right to left (for RH golfers). Shots in the "down" group, where the shot is being hit downhill or when the ball is below your feet will curve left to right (for RH golfers).

Uphill Shots

The first consideration in preparing for an uphill shot is club selection. Club selection will be affected by the severity of the slope and how high the green is in relation to the position of your ball. The slope of the hill will add effective loft to your club thus increasing the loft of a 7-iron to that of an 8- or even a 9-iron. If the green is higher than the position of your ball you will need to select more club (a less lofted club) in order to get your shot to fly all the way to the green before hitting the ground. The basic guidelines for club selection on an uphill shot are to use at least one more club than you would for a shot of the same distance on flat terrain.

Fig. 8.5. Set-up position for an uphill shot.

Also, when the green is above the level of your ball, use one more club for every 20 feet of elevation so that the shot will carry all the way onto the green (Figure 8.4). In your pre-shot routine, aim/align to the right of your target (for RH golfers) to compensate for the natural right to left curvature of the shot and for the tendency to sometimes pull the shot. Put a little more weight on your downhill foot and allow your shoulders to follow the slope of the hill. To prevent hitting the ball thin or topping it, play the ball forward in your stance toward your uphill foot (Figure 8.5). Make a practice swing and notice where your club contacts the ground and make an adjustment in ball position if necessary.

Ball Above Your Feet

When the ball is higher than your feet, your hands will be higher than normal which will flatten your swing plane. This also sets the toe of the club higher than normal. Both of these factors produce a shot that curves from right to left (for RH golfers). The more severe the slope, the more severely the shot will curve to the left. Aim and align accordingly. With the ball above your feet it is important to get your weight set correctly for good balance. Set your weight so that you lean into the hill slightly and place more weight on the balls of your feet. After you get your weight set comfortably and you feel balanced, simply allow your arms to hang naturally from your shoulders to establish the correct distance that the club and the ball should be from your body. Also, due to the fact that you are leaning slightly into the hill and the slope of the hill moves the ball closer to your body than normal, you will need to choke down on the grip of the club (Figure 8.6). Take a couple of practice swings to determine how far to choke down on the club so that you do not stick the club in the ground or miss the ball entirely when you swing.

Fig. 8.6. Set-up position for a ball that is above your feet.

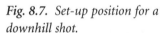

Fig. 8.7. Set-up position for a downhill shot.

Downhill Shots

Shots that are played from a downhill lie take effective loft off of the face of the club at address. To compensate, use a more lofted club to make sure that you get the shot airborne and to adjust for the fact that the shot will carry farther because the green is below the level of your ball. Aim the clubface and align your body to the left of your target (for RH golfers) to allow the shot to take its natural curvature back toward the target. Put a little more weight on your downhill foot and allow your shoulders to follow the slope of the hill. By playing the ball more toward the uphill foot you will avoid making contact with the ground prior to contacting the ball (Figure 8.7). With a nice balanced set-up, try to maintain your swing triangle and swing parallel to the slope to allow the shot to get up into the air without unnecessary effort on your part.

Fig. 8.8. Set-up position for a ball that is below your feet.

Ball Below Your Feet

Hitting a shot when the ball is below your feet is arguably the most difficult of the four side-hill shots. The best bet here is to choose one or two clubs more than normal so that you can make a shorter, smoother swing. Also, the extra length of the club allows your arms to hang more comfortably and naturally without feeling like you have to reach for the ball. To maintain your balance better, allow your weight to move more toward your heels and into the slope (Figure 8.8). When the ball is below your feet, your swing plane will tend to be more upright and there is a tendency for your weight to move out over the ball on the forward swing. If this happens, your swing path will come from outside across your intended target line. This combined with the fact that the toe of the club is lower than the heel of the club creates a shot that curves from left to right (for RH players). Aim and align parallel left of your target to allow the shot to curve back toward your target naturally.

Sand Play

Playing from the sand strikes more fear in the heart of some golfers than any other shot in the game. These same golfers often marvel at how the tour players "make sand shots look so easy." The ironic part of this statement is that sand shots *are* easy. They are made difficult due to poor technique and a lack of confidence. While every other shot in golf requires solid contact with the ball in the center of the clubface, the club does not even touch the ball when hitting from a greenside bunker. Instead, you will intentionally "miss" the ball. The idea is contact the sand from two, to as much as six, inches behind the ball and let the displaced sand carry the ball onto the green. After you have had a chance to practice and gain more confidence in playing from the sand, you will sometimes find that a missed approach shot that lands in a greenside bunker is actually preferable to some other trouble shots around the green, such as hitting out of deep rough.

Greenside Sand Play

Most of the sand traps (bunkers) that you will encounter on the course are located near or around the green. These bunkers are strategically placed to guard the green and increase the difficulty of the hole. When you find that your approach shot has landed in a greenside bunker you should first survey the situation to decide the best plan for getting the ball out of the sand and onto the green. Before you attempt the shot consider these variables, which will influence your club selection and your swing.

1. What is the texture of the sand? Is it fine, fluffy, coarse, wet, dry, etc?
2. Is the ball sitting up on top of the sand, or is it partially or completely buried in the sand?
3. How high is the lip of the bunker that must be cleared?
4. How far is the ball from the hole?
5. How much green do you have to work with between the fringe and the hole?

Club Selection

The sand wedge was designed specifically to make bunker shots easier. Gene Sarazen invented the club back in 1932 and used it to win the British Open that same year. Sarazen got the idea for the sand wedge from observing the way the flaps on the tail of an airplane caused the nose of the plane to lift as the flaps went down. He went home and soldered a thick flange on the rear of the sole of his 9-iron (Peper, 1999). This lowered the trailing edge of the sole relative to the leading edge, creating what is referred to as "bounce" (see Chapter 6 and Figure 6.1). This bounce is what allows the rear of the club to strike the sand first, causing the club to bounce out of the sand rather than digging into the sand. You can adjust the bounce by how much you open the clubface. This allows you to adjust how deeply the club will penetrate the sand so that it to slides under the ball trapping a layer of sand between the ball and the clubface (Figure 8.9). You can purchase sand wedges with soles of varying thickness and varying amounts of bounce to fit your ability level, or the type of sand that you normally play from at your course.

Set-Up and Aim/Alignment

The set-up for a greenside sand shot is similar to a short, high pitch shot. Start by aiming your feet, hips and shoulders on a line to the left of your target (for RH golfers) with the ball positioned just inside of the heel of your front foot. Then dig your feet into the sand just a little to

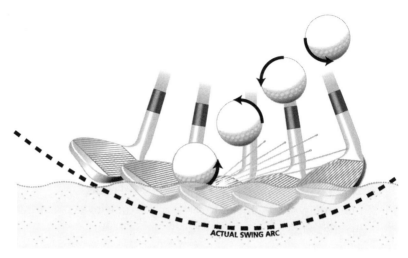

Fig. 8.9. *Illustration of how the club should contact the sand 2–3 inches behind the ball. The club takes a cut of sand about 6 inches long, sliding under the ball trapping a layer of sand between the clubface and the ball.*

help establish a firm footing. You may find it helpful to put the weight more toward the inside of your feet for better balance. Digging your feet into the sand will also allow you to "legally" test the sand. Is the sand coarse or fine? Is it wet? How much sand is underneath the ball, etc.? If you were to test the surface of the hazard—a sand bunker is a hazard—in any other manner, such as touching the sand with your club before starting your swing, you would under Rule 13-4, a and b, incur a penalty of two strokes in stroke play or loss of the hole in match play (USGA Rule Book, 2003).

Fig. 8.10. *Set-up for a greenside bunker shot when the ball is sitting up on the sand.*

Grip

Ordinarily, you would take your grip prior to setting-up for a shot, however, sand shots require you to alter this order slightly. When the ball is sitting up on top of the sand you will want to take a shallow cut of sand. For this type of shot, start by opening the clubface so that the trailing edge of the flange will contact the sand first, allowing the club to slide under the ball and give you the maximum amount of bounce (Figure 8.10). Be sure that you open the clubface *before* taking your grip. Merely turning the clubface open with your hands without regripping the club will simply bring the clubface back to square as the club enters the sand. This would allow the leading edge of the club to dig too deeply into the sand. It is important that you keep the clubhead accelerating through the shot into a nice high follow-through. Otherwise you could miss your main objective, which is to get the ball out of the bunker and onto the green.

Stroke

Rather than worrying about contacting the exact spot where you will hit the sand, simply imagine an area *two to three inches behind the ball* which provides you with a large target and a comfortable margin for error (Figure 8.11). You may find it helpful to imagine that the ball is sitting on a dollar bill with the ball centered on George Washington's portrait. The club will take a shallow cut in the sand beginning at the back of the dollar bill exiting near the front. This produces a divot in the sand about six inches long beginning about three inches behind the ball (Figure 8.12).

The backswing should begin slowly with the arms and shoulders moving together in one motion. Allow the wrists to hinge naturally as the swing reaches waist high. When the ball is sitting up on the sand, your back swing should be shallower, more u-shaped (Figure 8.13). A more shallow swing helps the club to bounce rather than dig into the sand. The length of the backswing and the club used will dictate the distance of the shot. Experiment with different length backswings in practice to learn distance control. Also, experiment with your 9-iron and your other wedges from the sand. When you are faced with a

Fig. 8.11. Contact the sand 2 to 3 inches behind the ball.

Fig. 8.12. Imagine that your ball is sitting on George Washington's picture and contact the sand 2 to 3 inches behind the ball, sliding the club under the ball and taking a 6-inch cut of sand.

Fig. 8.13. U-shaped swing when ball is sitting up on top of the sand and a more V-shaped swing when the ball is buried or partially buried in the sand.

sand shot that has to fly more than 10 or 15 yards, you will need to use your pitching wedge or 9-iron to get the necessary distance. Practicing with different clubs will give you more options and better distance control from the sand.

Accelerating the club through the sand into a nice, high follow through is necessary to ensure that you get the ball out of the sand on the first try. An accelerating swing that impacts the sand two to three inches behind the ball with the trailing edge of the club will produce a "thump" sound as the clubhead slides underneath the ball and bounces out of the sand carrying the ball out on a layer of sand. The fact that you have such a large margin of error (i.e., you can make contact with the sand as much as six inches behind the ball) is what makes the sand shot "easy." A sand shot only becomes difficult when you allow negative thoughts to alter the tempo of your swing. When this happens it will cause you either to lift up and blade the ball across the green or to decelerate the club and bury it in the sand.

Buried Lies

Sometimes you will find that because the ball landed in the sand on a steep trajectory or the sand is very soft your ball may be partially

buried (a "fried egg" lie) or completely buried (Figure 8.14). When your ball is partially buried in the sand, address the ball with a square clubface so that the leading edge of the club will contact the sand first (Figure 8.15) and dig under the ball, popping it out on a heavy layer of sand. When your ball is buried more deeply in the sand, close the clubface slightly to take an even deeper cut of sand and counteract the sand by twisting the clubface open as the hosel of the club enters the sand first.

Fig. 8.14. Ball sitting up on the sand; partially buried—"fried egg"; buried lie in the sand.

For both the "fried egg" and buried lie, you need to play the ball back more in your stance. The deeper the ball is buried, the farther back you play it in your stance. Playing the ball back in your stance and moving the hands slightly in front of the ball promote a more upright, v-shaped swing (Figure 8.13). This allows the club to dig deep enough to get under the ball. Make a much longer swing than you think is necessary. Heavy contact with the sand will slow the club considerably. The steeper swing and deeper cut of sand produced with this type of shot causes the ball to pop out on a lower trajectory with less backspin. Take this into consideration and allow more room for the shot to roll once it hits the green. From a buried lie the goal is not trying to get the ball close to the hole, but to get the ball out of the sand and somewhere on the green. If your next shot is a putt, your buried sand shot was a success.

Wet Sand

Playing from wet sand may be easier than playing from dry, fluffy sand because the club will slide under the ball more easily in wet sand. The density of wet sand causes the club to bounce more than it will in dry sand. Also, from wet sand, a shot will have less backspin and roll more than a shot from dry sand. For these reasons it would be better to use a lob wedge which has less bounce than a sand wedge. With less bounce, the lob wedge will be less likely to bounce too much which would cause it to skid into the ball and blade it over the green. The extra loft will give the shot more needed spin. Because of the extra resistance of dense, wet sand you will need to swing a little harder than you would for a similar shot from dry sand in order to keep the club accelerating through the shot.

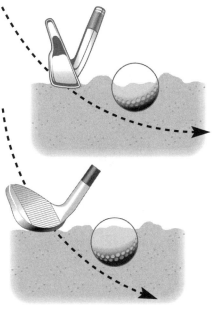

Fig. 8.15. How the club should contact the sand when the ball is buried in the sand.

Fairway Bunkers

Many years ago, some sadistic soul came up with the idea of putting sand bunkers on the edge of the fairway far from the green. Unfortunately, some modern golf course architects have taken this idea to the extreme. Rather than placing fairway bunkers to guard a dogleg or force the golfer to lay up, these architects sometimes have a fairway bunker running the entire length of the hole.

Club Selection

If your ball is sitting up on the sand you will want to use one more club than you would for a fairway shot from the same distance. This will not always be possible because the club must have enough loft to get the

Fig. 8.16. Set-up for a fairway sand shot.

ball over the lip of the bunker. You want to make a shallow, u-shaped swing that contacts the ball first, sweeping it off the surface of the sand. A fairway wood with its wide, rounded sole works well when you have a long shot from a fairway bunker. The sole of the fairway wood will slide through, rather than dig into, the sand. If your ball is in a buried lie you probably will not be able to reach the green. Instead, use your sand wedge to blast the ball safely out into the fairway, and leave yourself with a safe shot to the green on your next shot.

Grip

Use your normal, full swing. You may want to increase the tension in the last three fingers of your left hand. Also, choke down on the club the same amount that you dig your feet into the sand.

Aim/Alignment

Normal aim and alignment, parallel left of your target (for RH golfers).

Set-Up

Dig your feet in slightly with the inside of your feet slightly lower than the outside to help stabilize your feet in the sand. Position the ball a little forward of center in your stance so that your swing can sweep the ball off the sand (Figure 8.16).

Stroke

Start the club back slowly, making a normal full backswing. Avoid the temptation to swing too hard. Accelerate the forward swing smoothly so that you maintain your balance, and allow the club to do the work. If you contact the ball first, sweeping it off of the sand, you will get almost the same distance that you would from the fairway. Therefore, there is no need to put any extra effort into the swing. Simply use one more club than you would for a shot of the same distance from the fairway. You may not be Tiger Woods, but you will be pleased with the results.

Shots from the Rough

Shots from the rough vary in difficulty depending on the length of the grass, the type of grass, and the obstacles or hazards that might be between your ball and the green.

Club Selection

The length of the grass and the distance to the pin will dictate your club selection. When the grass is long and the ball is nestled down in the grass you will need to use a heavier club with plenty of loft to get the ball out of the rough. Some grass, such as Bermuda, can be so thick that it is difficult to get the club though it, making it next to impossible to get the ball out and onto the green. In this case, your best option is to simply get the ball back in the fairway and go for the green with your next shot. If the ball is not sitting down too far in the grass (at least half of the ball is above the grass), you should be able to get the club on the ball and advance the shot with little difficulty.

For this shot, select one less club than you would for a fairway shot from the same distance because of the "flyer" effect caused when grass gets caught between the ball and the clubface. The grass that is trapped between the ball and the clubface reduces the spin on the ball causing it to come out "hot" and roll farther once it hits the ground. If you are close enough for your shot to hit the green, play for the front of the green so that the ball does not roll off the back of the green. Because of the reduced spin on the ball from this type of lie, trying to make the shot purposely curve left or right will be difficult at best.

Fig. 8.17. Shot from shallow rough using a fairway wood.

If you are faced with a long shot from the rough and the ball is not sitting down in the grass, using a fairway wood will be easier than a long iron (Figure 8.17). The fairway wood has a wide, rounded sole with a shorter hosel and a lower center of gravity. The wide, rounded sole of a fairway wood allows it to glide through the grass with less resistance than a long iron which tends to dig and cut into the grass more. The shorter hosel of a fairway wood also provides less resistance to the grass, which tends to grab the hosel and twist the clubface into a closed position. A long iron will get twisted more, which de-lofts the clubface, making it difficult to get the ball up out of the rough, causing the shot to fly low and left of the intended target. The loft of lower

center of gravity and loft of a fairway wood also makes it easier to hit the shot with a higher trajectory and more backspin so that the ball lands softer with less roll.

Grip

Use your normal, full swing grip. Because the grass will try to twist the club as it moves through the grass, you may want to use a slightly firmer grip with your left hand, and set the clubface slightly open before you take your grip. Do not hold the club too tightly though. A grip that is too tight may cause you to swing too hard and too fast with a hacking swing *at* the ball rather than a smooth swing *through* the ball.

Aim/Alignment

Aim the clubface and align your body toward the widest part of the fairway or green. Because shots from the rough have less spin, the shot will have less curvature left or right. You simply want to aim for the largest, widest landing area possible in order to get the ball back safely into play.

Set-Up

As you address the ball, hold the clubhead above the grass to prevent the grass catching it on your backswing (Figure 8.18). Also, if your club touches the grass as you address the ball and the ball moves, you incur a one-stroke penalty under rule 18-2, b and c, (USGA Rule Book, 2003). If the ball is sitting down in the grass play the ball in the center of your stance. The deeper the ball sits in the grass, the farther back in your stance you will play the ball to produce a descending swing arc. If the ball is sitting up more in the rough, and you are using a longer club, play the ball forward in your stance for a more shallow swing arc that sweeps the ball out of the rough.

Fig. 8.18. For shots from deep rough, address the ball with the club up out of the grass.

Stroke

In deep rough, playing the ball back in your stance allows you to make a more vertical, v-shaped, backswing (Figure 8.13). This will help you avoid catching the club in the grass as it goes back—throwing your timing off. The forward swing should follow this same vertical arc coming down in order to avoid catching too much grass between the ball and the clubface, which could prevent you from advancing the ball out of the rough. The forward swing should be firm, accelerating the club down and through the ball. The goal is to get the ball out of the rough and into the fairway, not to get the ball on the green. There is no pressure to make a miracle shot here. If you find that your ball is sitting up in the grass, make a more shallow u-shaped swing so that you avoid having the club go too deep into the grass; either passing under the ball or just catching it with the top edge of the clubface.

Wind

How many times have you played well on a windy day? Probably not very often, but take heart, even the tour players have a difficult time in the wind. Patience, and a positive attitude go a long way when playing under windy conditions. Try to remember that everyone else has to play under the same conditions and their scores will also be higher than normal. Once you have your mental focus in the proper perspective, the physical part will be easier to control.

Two areas that you want to focus on when playing in windy conditions are balance and tempo. By widening your stance you will effectively lower your center of gravity, making it easier to maintain your balance. Concentrate on your tempo on each shot throughout the round. Wind tends to cause you to speed up your swing and throws your timing off. After a bad shot, and before you start the back nine, take a couple of minutes to make a conscious effort to refocus on swing tempo and a positive attitude. One of the most effective ways to help with tempo is to use one more club than you think you will need for the shot. Knowing that you have plenty of club relaxes you, allowing you to make a nice, smooth swing rather than feeling like you need to really muscle the shot.

Determining the velocity and direction of the wind is accomplished in different ways. Looking at how hard and in what direction the flag is flapping is one method. Another method is to toss a few blades of grass into the air, watching its direction and how fast it moves. Because the ball will be flying on a higher trajectory than the flag and where you are standing, it would also be good to check the tops of nearby trees. Watch not only for wind speed and direction, but also check to see if the wind is swirling.

Headwind

Playing a shot into the wind requires you to keep the shot on a lower trajectory to reduce the effect of the wind and to avoid the ball ballooning up in the wind and getting knocked down. On your tee shots, tee the ball a little lower and try to sweep the ball off the tee. Teeing the ball too high will start the off on a trajectory that is too high, resulting in a short drive and leaving you with an approach shot that is beyond your range. For approach shots with an iron, play the ball back in your stance (Figure 8.3) and use at least one more club (a lower numbered club). Your follow through should be a little lower than normal, more like making a punch shot. This helps to keep the shot on a lower trajectory, and gives you the distance that you need without ruining your swing tempo. Hitting down hard on the back of the ball will create extra backspin causing the shot to fly higher into the wind.

Tailwind

Playing a shot with the wind at your back allows you to use a more lofted club than normal so that you can get the ball up and let the wind carry it toward your target. You may also get extra distance on this shot if the wind has dried the fairways and greens causing them to harden. Harder ground provides more bounce and roll once the ball hits. Experience will help you to judge more accurately the speed of the wind and which club you should use on a particular shot.

Crosswinds

Winds that blow across the direction of flight of your shot present more of a dilemma in trying to keep the ball in play. You basically have two options depending on your skill level, or preference: 1) you can curve the ball into the wind, or 2) you can aim well left or right of your target to compensate for the wind.

If you have the skill to shape your shots (make the shot intentionally curve left or right), it is best to curve the shot into the wind so that it will fly almost straight toward your target with a softer landing. If you have difficulty shaping your shots, you should aim and align so that your ball starts in the direction of the wind. Then let the wind carry the ball back toward your target or intended landing area. A word of caution on this, however. The ball will roll more in the direction of the wind once it hits the ground, which may cause it to roll out of the fairway or off the green.

With experience, your shot selection and confidence will improve when playing in windy conditions. By maintaining a positive attitude and good swing tempo you will find that you can often beat players whom you do not beat on calm days.

Stymied Shots

"Hey Bob, I found your ball, but you're not going to like it." Occasionally, your ball will end up in a position where you cannot make a normal right-handed swing. When this happens you have three options: 1) declare the ball unplayable, 2) make a left-handed swing, or 3) make a backward swing. Declaring the ball unplayable only allows you to move the ball two club lengths and requires that you take a penalty stroke under Rule 28 (USGA Rule Book, 2003). In order to avoid a penalty stroke you may want to try option 2 or 3. With either of these options you are merely trying to get the ball back in play while avoiding a penalty stroke. Avoid allowing your creativity or the desire to hit "the shot of your life" to overcome your common sense and tempt your to try a shot that is beyond your capabilities.

Left-Handed Swing

Making a left-handed swing at the ball actually offers you two options to advance the ball. The first option is to strike the ball with the back of the clubhead (Figure 8.19) using a lower lofted iron, usually a 3-iron. This creates a low, running shot that works if you have no obstacles and only fairway in your intended line of flight. Be careful with this option as the irregular shape of the back of some newer cast clubs may cause to ball to shoot off in an undesirable direction. The second option is to turn the toe of the club down (Figure 8.19) to strike the ball. Use a more lofted club that provides more surface area to contact the ball and pop the ball up and out into play.

Fig. 8.19. Left-handed swing from a stymied lie.

Fig. 8.20. Backward swing from a stymied lie.

Backward Swing

The backward swing is usually the easiest option for most people. Simply take a stance beside the ball with your feet together and your back facing the direction that you want the shot to go. Then choke down on the club with the grip against your forearm and make a short, stiff-armed backward swing (Figure 8.20). Making the same swing and cocking your wrist on the backswing can produce more momentum and advance the ball farther.

Practice the left-handed swing and the backward swing to see which method works best for you. Regardless of which method you use, keep in mind that the objective is simply to advance the ball to a position where you can play your next shot without interference. Only on rare occasion will you be able to get the ball on the green from one of these situations.

9 Practice and Practice Drills: Building Confidence and Consistency

The best way to eliminate errors in your golf game is through specific and diligent practice. The obvious benefit is that practice will help you build confidence in a more correct and more repeatable swing pattern—even under pressure. Practice will allow you to develop the ability to play by "feel," to feel the swing take place, rather than just to "hit the ball." What a great sensation it is to have confidence in your swing, knowing that you can make a delicate pitch shot over a sand bunker and land the ball softly, close to the hole—with only a short putt remaining for the match!

In practice, you can relax and work on your swing without the pressure that you may feel on the course. On the practice range there is no

Fig. 9.1. The practice range.

101

penalty if you make a poor shot. However, too many people feel that practice is time-consuming and is often boring. Yes, it does take time to improve your game. To help you deal with the time issue, try to shorten your sessions to 20–30 minutes of work done 2–3 times per week rather than spending hours at it. As for boredom, use your imagination; work on your visualization skills and use those clubs in your bag to heighten your interest by playing contests with yourself. To further emphasize the need for practice, you should keep in mind that relying solely on playing rounds of golf to improve your skills will limit your level of success. You may show some improvement, but you will ultimately reach a plateau from which your game never seems to improve. That in itself is not a bad thing if your goal is simply to get out and enjoy a round of golf on the weekend with your friends, with little regard as to the score. However, it is our contention that the majority of golfers have a real desire to improve. Some may even dream of having a game that would allow them to formally compete as an amateur or even on a professional tour. Regardless of whether you would like to improve one aspect of your game, improve your whole game, or improve enough to compete in formal competition, practice is essential in achieving your goal. It has been said before and bears repeating: practicing improves your game, develops your confidence, and golf then becomes even more enjoyable.

Practice with a Purpose

Practice is the basis for improving your game, and each practice shot you make should have a specific purpose or goal. Too often you will find golfers at a driving range just flailing away at ball after ball with no objective in mind other than to see how far they can hit. Immediately after each shot they rake another ball over and try to send this one farther than the last with little, if any, regard to a pre-shot routine or to the specific outcome of the shot. This type of practice only serves to establish and ingrain poor habits and swing fundamentals so deeply that it becomes extremely difficult to change them. Wiren (1992) admonishes that "any relationship between this kind of practice and score improvement is purely coincidental" (p. 112).

Instead of merely beating balls, you would do well to take a few seconds between each shot to reflect on how that swing felt, what the result of the shot was, and how the two were related. An attempt should be made to feel the swing, not to hit the ball. As Toski et al. (1984) explain, "You don't have to hit the ball. The hit is simply the result of the ball getting in the way of the clubhead as it passes through the impact area" (p. 23). We would advise you to follow a pre-shot routine with every practice shot you hit. Consequently, when you find yourself on the golf course, the shots you make will be approached just as you have practiced, and you will see that there is a very direct relationship between how you practice and how you play.

Perhaps the name "driving range," which conjures images of hitting the ball 300 yards downrange with the driver, is part of the problem. Wiren (1992) suggests that the name be changed to "practice range" or "learning center" to promote the image of a purposeful place to practice the golf swing rather than a place merely to "hit" golf balls. While a commercial range is convenient in that you do not have to provide your own practice balls—and you do not have to pick them up after you hit them!—it is not the most conducive setting for working on correcting your swing. The large numbers of people present, all walking around, swinging clubs and talking, tend to detract from your ability to concentrate fully, thus reducing the effectiveness of your practice. A better alternative might be to get off to an area such as an unused football field or park where you are by yourself, without distractions, so that you can work on the fundamentals of grip, alignment, set-up, and a smooth, balanced swing. Another good place for practice is a practice net in your backyard or in your basement. Some of these nets are inexpensive, and they allow you to work on your swing when time and/or weather are limiting factors. Such workouts might also be good times to videotape your swing so that you can see if you have been successful in correcting a swing flaw.

Types of Practice

Just as there is more than one type of place to practice, there is more than one type of practice. The most common types of practices include pre-round warm-up, process-oriented, product-oriented, game-simulated, and mental imagery.

Pre-Round Warmup

Your pre-round warmup should start with a few stretching exercises to get your back, shoulder, arm and leg muscles ready to make the good full turn that will produce a smooth swing. Stretching will also reduce the chances of an injury. Next, take a few easy swings with two or three clubs, or a specially weighted club, to further prepare your muscles for a full swing. The warmup session can be used to get a feel for the swing

and to establish good tempo. You only need to hit 25 to 30 balls, starting with a short iron and working up to the driver for the last five balls or so. Be especially concerned with establishing your tempo, the pace of the swing which feels most comfortable. By focusing on your tempo during this practice session, you can avoid the tendency to swing faster as you hit more balls, especially with the driver. Try to accept that this is really a warmup session, and it is not a good time to be modifying your swing mechanics. How-

Fig. 9.2. Pre-round warmup.

ever, this *is* a good time to review your swing keys, to both remind yourself of what you have worked on and to reaffirm them in respect to your mind set. After you have finished hitting shots on the practice range, try five or six sand shots if there is a practice bunker. Then move over to the practice green to hit a few chip shots, and work on putts of various lengths to get a feel for the speed of the greens.

Process-Oriented Practice

Process-oriented practice sessions (Bunker and Owens, 1984) are usually held in conjunction with, and precede, product-oriented practices. Process-oriented practice is directed at establishing a feel for your swing and the contribution of the different body parts to the swing. This is the time to break down the swing into its various parts and to correct flaws or bad habits so that they do not become ingrained or habitual. You may best accomplish this through the use of various drills that concentrate on some aspect of your swing that needs work. Suppose you are having difficulty with your weight shift, i.e., you tend to finish with your weight more on your dominant side in the follow-through. There are two good drills to promote a proper weight shift: the crossed arms drill (Figures 9.4, 9.5, 9.6) and the "swing-click-step-swing" drill (Figures 9.15, 9.16, 9.17, 9.18). By using one or both of these drills, you will be better able to acquire a feel for the entire swing, one which encourages a weight transfer to the target side and a balanced finish position. When you are concentrating on the "feel" of a certain body part it will sometimes interfere with the swing's timing as a whole, which will affect the outcome of the shot. This should not concern you at this time, because getting "… the feel of a swing motion, or making the desired motion technically efficient, is the most important objective during the process-orientation phase of practice" (Bunker and Owens, 1984, p. 139). The drills used in process-oriented practice are the building blocks for beginning golfers' swings and the repair glue for the top amateurs'and professionals' swings.

Product-Oriented Practice

Product-oriented practice sessions (Bunker and Owens, 1984) usually follow process-oriented sessions. They shift the focus from the feel of the swing to the actual result of the shot. The goal for each shot shifts from the internally centered feel of the swing (or some part of the swing) to the ultimate outcome of the shot; i.e., did the shot have the intended trajectory, did it go the intended distance, and did it land within the intended landing area? In the product-oriented phase of practice, as in an actual round of golf, you pick out a specific target for each shot and an intended trajectory (to the left or to the right). You then set up and execute the shot without concerning yourself with all the mechanics of the swing. You have to trust that the swing you built in the process-oriented phase of practice will be repeatable; now you are thinking only of target and tempo, otherwise you will run into the problem commonly referred to as "paralysis from analysis"—thinking too much.

Top Ten Tips and Practice Guidelines

1. The proper attitude is important for practice to be productive. Practice should be viewed as something you "want " to do versus something you "have" to do. If you do not want to practice, you will not have the focus that is necessary to improve your swing. Try to make your practices enjoyable so that you will want to practice.

2. Place extra clubs or paint some lines on the ground to help ensure that your alignment and the position of the ball in your stance are correct. You may even consider asking someone to stand behind you at address to verify that what you think you "see" as the correct line is, in fact, the actual line.

3. Begin your practice with the short irons, making short, easy swings, and progress up to longer swings, working on feel and tempo. Many golfers then choose to hit the even-numbered clubs one practice session and change to the odd-numbered clubs the following time out. Next, hit a handful of shots with each of your woods, finishing with the driver. Complete your practice with some work on and around the green.

4. A good practice technique is to hit one club, starting with a short iron—preferably your pitching wedge or sand wedge—and stay with that club until you hit what in your terms is a good shot. At that point you may move on, in order, to the next club in your bag, getting increasingly longer. The positive aspect of this drill is that you will end up spending a lot of time on the clubs which have been the most difficult to hit in the past, while at the same time honing your technique.

5. A good variation of the above drill is to put a little pressure on yourself while you practice. Pull out 30 practice balls and start with the wedge. Once again, you cannot move on to the next club until you hit that "good shot." Now see how far through your bag you can get before you have hit all 30 balls! A note of importance at this point is that you should hit every ball during practice just as you do on the course—with your pre-shot routine.

6. As you progress upward through your set of clubs, attempt to learn the specific distance that you can hit each club.

7. Occasionally work on hitting draws, fades, and high and low shots so that if you need to hit one of these shots to avoid or get out of trouble during a round, you will have some confidence in your ability to do so.

8. Practice all phases of your game, not just your strengths. Devote some extra work to your weaknesses in order to round out your game. Remember that the short game (less than a full swing) is approximately two-thirds of your scoring and should receive two-thirds of your attention!

9. Your practice will be more productive if you have shorter, more frequent practice sessions. Instead of practicing once a week for two or three hours, a better approach would be to practice two to five times a week for 20–45 minutes. These shorter, more frequent practice sessions will help ingrain swing patterns into your long-term memory bank and make them potentially more repeatable, even under pressure situations.

10. Try to finish your practice sessions on a positive note by working on your favorite part of the game or hitting with your favorite club, thinking only of tempo. The memory of a successful practice will carry over into your game, giving you positive images from which to draw.

Game-Simulated Practice

Another important method of practice is game-simulated practice. By simulating play, you take into account the many variables, both mental and physical, that occur during a round but are generally not present on the practice tee. This method is effective because as Straub (1980) related, "…practicing a skill must occur in conditions as close to game conditions as possible. This encourages the transfer of the skill" (p. 21). Game-simulated practice occurs on or around the practice green or on the course itself and can be done alone or with others. Start at the practice green with chipping; lay out several balls at various distances and practice getting all of your chip shots within a three-foot radius of the hole. Pretend that each shot is one you would make in an actual round so that you will have a realistic shot at one-putting to save par. Another goal might be to actually chip 3 out of 10 shots into the hole before you move to the next part of your practice.

This same goal can be used when working on long (30 feet or more) putts; that is, try to get all of the putts within a two- to three-foot radius of the hole in order to have a decent chance of making your next putt. On shorter putts the goal may be to make 3 out of 10 of your 20-foot putts, 5 out of 10 of the 10-foot putts and 8 out of 10 of the four-foot putts. Remember, this is game-simulated practice; therefore, you want to prepare for each shot as carefully as you would in an actual round. If you are practicing with a friend or friends, compete with one another to see who can chip the ball the closest to the target or who can putt out in the fewest number of putts, with the winner of each hole choosing the next hole. This type of practice puts you in a very game-like situation and makes practice more fun. If you have time early in the morning or late in the evening when there are not very many people on the course, an excellent form of game-simulated practice is to go out and play with two or three balls. Hit three tee shots and choose the best one; then, hit three balls near that spot from different situations, e.g., the fairway, the rough, or a side-hill lie. Choose one of those shots and hit three balls near that spot from different situations and so on until you finish the hole. This will allow you to practice many of the types of shots you might will face on the course and will help to instill more confidence when you have to execute these shots in an actual round.

Mental Practice

A final type of practice is mental imagery (visualization). Visualization has received much attention in the past few years as more and more elite athletes have begun to consult with sports psychologists after seeing the positive results of mental practice. Essentially, visualization works in this manner: our brains cannot distinguish between something that really happens from something that we imagine to have happened. So "...when the actual competition begins, mentally-prepared athletes (have)...seen it countless times before—in their minds" (Penn State, 1992, p. 4). The use of visualization can and should take place on the golf course as well as in places away from the course where you can sit for several minutes and mentally rehearse your swing or playing strategy. With some practice and experience at this technique, the images may become "...so clear and vivid as to reproduce visual, tactual, auditory, motor, and even emotional reactions" (Straub, 1980, p. 25). A good example of this type of practice can be seen when watching Olympic luge competitors with their eyes closed going through the twists and turns of the course in their mind prior to making their run. In addition to using visualization to practice your golf swing or game strategy at home, it is very important to employ it during your pre-shot routine. "It can [then] be a little bit like your best friend, a comfort in times of stress—a security blanket" (Coop, 1993, p. 59). As you stand behind the ball to pick a line to the target and find an intermediate target, visualize the shot leaving the ground and the shape and trajectory the ball will take as it flies to the target. By employing visualization while at home and in your pre-shot routine, you can help to erase negative thoughts ("don't hit it in that lake on the right!") and replace them with positive thoughts ("150 yards with a nice draw landing next to the pin"), thus building confidence in your swing and the ability to handle pressure when you play.

Practice Drills

The Importance of Practice Drills

How many times have you heard that "practice doesn't make perfect; perfect practice makes perfect"? Probably more times than you care to have heard it; yet, how much of your practice is devoted to drills and how much is spent just "beating balls"? As stated before, the more you practice your swing using a poor technique, the more deeply this swing flaw will become ingrained into that blueprint you have created in your mind, making it infinitely harder to correct. Breaking your swing down through the use of drills in order to build good swing habits is necessary if you desire to improve your game and advance to a higher level of play.

> Properly incorporated into your practice sessions, they [drills] can greatly speed your improvement, because they can help you use your time productively,…[and they] force you to use the correct muscles in the swing instead of just standing there beating balls and perfecting your mistakes (Toski et al., 1984, p. 294).

This section outlines some of the many practice drills that are available to help you develop a more efficient, more repeatable swing. If you would like to learn more about other drills, some excellent references include:

1. Ballard, 1981
2. Hebron, 1984
3. Leadbetter, 1990
4. Leadbetter, 1993
5. Leadbetter, 1997
6. National Golf Foundation, 1994
7. Pelz, 1999
8. Toski et al., 1984

Posture Drill

Stand erect and place a club against your spine so that it touches between your shoulder blades and the base of your spine. Hold the club in place with either hand. Next, flex your knees and bend forward from the

Fig. 9.3. Posture drill.

hips while keeping your weight over your knees and the balls of your feet. As your shoulders move forward, your hips will move back. If you bend with your shoulders or back, the club will not stay in contact with both points on your spine. Just allow your arm to hang naturally and comfortably (Figure 9.3). This drill aids in assuming your setup position with good erect posture, rather than a hunched or slumped posture.

Crossed Arms Swing Drill

This drill incorporates many parts of the golf swing. Beginners should spend a great amount of time trying it out and establishing a comfort level with the drill. Stand in your normal address position and, instead of holding a club in your hands, put your dominant hand on the front of your target shoulder and your target hand on the front of your dominant shoulder—hence the crossed arms drill (Figure 9.4). In your backswing position, you will turn your back to the target—on a full swing you will attempt to create a 90° angle between your shoulder girdle and the target line—with your chest (more accurately your "center," about

Figs. 9.4–9.6. Crossed arms drill.

where your sternum is) over your dominant heel (Figure 9.4). Your hips should turn about half as much as your shoulders do, approximately 45°. You should find yourself still inside the foundation you created with your legs at address; in other words, you did not move your weight laterally to a spot outside your dominant foot. You should allow your head to swivel if necessary to allow the shoulders to rotate; at that point, your target knee will point to some imaginary spot behind the golf ball's position at address.

During the forward swing, the angles you created at address (through your hips and knees) should still exist, and you will move from a "target shoulder under the chin" position to a "dominant shoulder under the chin" position. The forward swing rotation of the big muscles will end in the finish position (Figure 9.6). In the finish, your target side bears the brunt of your body weight (your body's center will then be over your target foot), while your navel and your dominant knee point to the target (the toe of your dominant foot touches the ground). You can spend much time working on swing fundamentals with this drill, beginning with body angles at address, and including balance and the concept of "center" positioning during the backswing and through to the finish.

Alignment and Swing Path Drill

Place a wooden 2×4 parallel to your intended line of flight. To overcome any initial fears that you may have of hitting the 2×4 when you attempt this drill, start by making short swings a few inches from the board and little by little increase the size of your swing while gradually moving your club closer to the board. As you become more comfortable with this, practice hitting balls from next to the board so that the toe of your club is about two inches from the board at address (Figure 9.7). This drill will aid you in establishing proper alignment to your target, in visualizing the swing path to your target, and in "feeling" the correct inside-to-inside swing path.

Fig. 9.7. Alignment and swing path drill.

Tempo Drills

1. **Hold at the top then swing drill** – Make a full backswing and pause at the top before you begin your downswing. This drill will help you to avoid making a backswing that is too fast, and it will allow you to consciously

be aware of the position of your hands and the club at the top of your backswing. The pause at the top also aids in developing a slower change of direction in the downswing. This will keep your arms swinging down on the inside of the swing path rather than spinning out with the shoulders and getting the club outside of the intended path.

2. **Full swing, but variable speed drill** – Make full swings with a 5-iron or a 7-iron, but control the swing speed so that the ball will only go about 25 percent of your normal distance for that club. About every five shots, increase your swing speed gradually until your shots are going 100 percent of your normal distance.

3. **Swing with your feet together drill** – Start out making half swings, progressing up to full swings with your feet close together (at the most, three or four inches apart) and the ball positioned off the inside of your target heel. This drill: (a) helps to reduce tension in your arms and upper body and allows the swing triangle created by your arms and shoulders to coordinate rotation and balance with your legs—all keys to good tempo: (b) forces you to maintain the angles of the spine and dominant knee in order to make solid contact with the ball and maintain your balance: and (c) forces you to swing the club rather than hit at the ball, another key ingredient to balance (Figures 9.8, 9.9, 9.10).

Figs. 9.8–9.10. Swing with your feet together drill.

Figs. 9.11–9.12. Toe up to toe up drill.

Arm and Hand Release Drills

1. **Toe up to toe up drill** – From the 1/4 swing checkpoint position (Figure 4.4) swing through the hitting area and stop when your club is again parallel to the ground—a mirror image of the previous position. At that point, the toe of your club should again be pointing to the sky, more preferably beginning to rotate towards the horizon. Accomplishing these swing positions allows your hands and arms to release naturally through the contact area with the ball, preventing blocking off the shot. Try hitting some shots with this drill (Figures 9.11 and 9.12).

2. **9-3 tee down drill** – Put a tee in the grip end of your club and make swings where the wrists cock as the hands move up to the 9 o'clock position in the backswing. Then allow the wrists to uncock natuarally on the downswing and recock on the follow-through as the hands come up

Figs. 9.13–9.14. Tee down drill.

to the 3 o'clock position. At the top of your backswing and follow-through, the tee in the end of the grip should point down toward the target line. This drill helps you to develop a feel for your forearms releasing and the clubhead rotating as the wrist cocks, uncocks, and recocks during the swing (Figures 9.13, 9.14).

Weight Transfer Drills

1. **Door stop or extra club drill** – Place a wooden door stop or the grip end of an extra club under the outside of your dominant foot as you make a few practice swings or hit a few balls. This drill will help you to develop a feel for rotating your weight around your dominant leg rather than making a lateral shift to the outside of your dominant foot.

2. **Swing-click-step-swing drill** – Take your normal address position, then make a ½ to ¾ backswing. Pause at the top of your backswing and click your target foot to your dominant foot, so that your weight is now transferred to your dominant foot (Figures 9.15, 9.16, 9.17, 9.18). Now step back toward your target with your target foot (try to put your target foot in its original address position), transferring your weight to your target foot. As your weight is transferring to your target side, begin your downswing. Be sure to finish in a balanced follow-through position, facing your target with your weight on your target foot. Practicing this drill is good for getting your weight transferred correctly and for beginning the swing from the ground up.

Figs. 9.15–9.18.
Swing-click-step-
swing drill.

Staying Behind the Ball Drill

Have a partner stand in front of you as you take your set-up position and place the grip end of their club next to your forehead (Figure 9.19). Make an easy swing and see if your head stays behind their club (but does not touch it) until after impact with the ball. If you stay behind the ball throughout the swing, your head will be in the position it should be during the golf swing.

Both practicing and practicing drills, those described in this text or others you may encounter in golf literature, increases your capacity to feel your golf swing. Only through practice can you then gain confidence and consistency, keys to improving your playing skills.

Fig. 9.19. Staying behind the ball drill.

10 Course Management: Putting It All Together

Many golf teachers emphasize four key areas during their instruction: the short game, long game, mental game, and course management (McLean, 1996). Whether or not your aspirations to attain a specific level of play in golf afford you the opportunity to spend the time required to gain comparable expertise in each of these four areas of the game, course management should play a significant role in your game. Until now, your attention has been directed toward trying to build a golf swing that is repeatable and correcting swing flaws that were giving you problems. Now you are ready to move from the practice tee to the course and apply the swing that you have worked on so diligently. Before beginning your round, it would be helpful if you developed strategies for completing your round in the fewest possible strokes. The ability to devise and execute appropriate strategies for each hole—and each shot—will allow you to become a good "course manager." Effective course management skills offer you the potential to keep your scores low, perhaps surpassing other golfers who may have a better short game, a better long game, or even a stronger mental game than you do.

The following strategies will give you a skeleton or framework around which you may build your course management skills. Through trial and error, you will become more adept as you practice these skills. By talking with other golfers and watching their strategies, you can further advance your own course management capabilities.

Arrive Early

In order to get your round off to a good start, it is important to arrive at the course well before your scheduled starting time. Driving up at the last minute, running out to the first tee, and scrambling to check that you have all of the equipment you will need guarantees that you are unprepared both mentally and physically. Your mind will be focused on other things, including the hurried drive to the course. Your muscles will not be stretched or warmed sufficiently to enable you to make a good golf swing. The result of all of this will usually be a poor start; by the time your mind begins to focus on golf and your muscles get "loose," your score and your round may not be salvageable.

By arriving at the course 30–60 minutes before your starting time, you will be able to accomplish the mental and physical preparations that help you have a more successful and enjoyable round. It is better to start with the mental preparation so that your body will able to respond to a mental state that is relaxed, positive, and focused on golf. Your thoughts should include firm ideas for playing each hole and the round in general; key swing thoughts; and visualization of good tempo. One method for getting your mind relaxed and focused is to get a scorecard and find a quiet, comfortable place to sit and review it. Spend just a few minutes looking at the card in order to plan your strategy for each hole. Also, as you are sitting quietly, begin to plan how you will play your round (i.e., do you attack the course or play conservatively?), and try to form a couple of key swing thoughts to use during the round. A general rule of thumb to consider is this: divide the course into thirds; the first third is played conservatively to condition yourself to the environment and get your "game face" on; the middle third is played aggressively if the course, conditions, and your game that day permit; and the last third is played a bit less aggressively to prevent a serious "wreck," yet not as conservatively as you began the round.

The physical preparation begins with slowly stretching and warming the muscles before you start to swing a club. The "pre-round warmup" section of Chapter 9 suggests a routine to follow. As you evolve in this aspect of your game, you may develop a different routine of your own. Remember that while you are on the practice tee you are there only to warm up and develop good swing tempo, not to rebuild your swing. Therefore, limit yourself to hitting just a few balls with each club, focusing on the feel of the swing. In addition, pay attention to the natural curvature of your shots so that you can alter your game strategy if necessary. If your shots tend to be fading or drawing, do not fight this or try to alter it; instead, incorporate this curvature into your game strategy and work to make corrections during a later practice time. After warming up on the practice range, move to the practice green to develop a feel for the speed of the greens by making a few putts of varying lengths, beginning with putts of no more than two or three feet. Try using a target reduced in size—a coin for example—to make the hole appear much larger during your round. Finish by trying to imprint your mind with a feel for the speed of the greens. Remember, the two obstacles faced on the green are distance and direction; you must believe that distance (the speed of the putt) is uppermost in importance.

The Mental Game

After having some time to hit a few warm-up shots at the practice tee and to relax and plan your strategy for the round, you are ready to move to the first tee to begin your round. As you go to the tee, you should be physically prepared and mentally aware of the strategy you are going to use that day. Visualize the flight pattern of your shots and have a couple of swing thoughts to focus on during the round. While the physical warm-up is certainly important, the mental preparation is even more significant, since it focuses you on the three vital areas of playing the game that Toski et al., (1984) refer to as control of the game, control of your swing, and control of yourself.

Control of Your Game

Control of your game starts with matching the strengths and weaknesses of your game against the strengths and weaknesses of the course you are playing. To become a better course manager, you have to become a better self-manager. The first factor in achieving self-management is a knowledge of yourself, a realistic evaluation of what your swing can do and the shots you can play, of your abilities at the time you are playing—not last week, not next week, but now. You must [also] have a knowledge of the strengths and weaknesses of the golf course at the time you are playing it, which takes into account weather conditions, distance, hole layout and hazards (Toski et al., 1984, p. 274).

The scorecard that you picked up at the club's pro shop is your road map of the course. As you review the scorecard and to help you establish a game plan for the day, apply the knowledge of your shot patterns that you gained while warming up. If this is your first time at the course, use the scorecard to glean as much information about the course as you can, e.g., the length of the holes, potential hazards, doglegs, local rules, out of bounds, etc. By using the input obtained from your warm-up and the scorecard, you will be able to develop better course management skills and prepare better game plans which will help you keep your score closer to your true potential.

The tee shot is generally the longest shot on each hole; therefore, the possibilities of getting into trouble are greater. While a majority of golfers are more concerned with obtaining more distance off the tee, the lower handicap golfers are more concerned with "position" on their tee shots. "Position golf is practical golf; power golf is poor golf" (Toski et al., 1984, p. 274). Or as Harvey Penick said in his *Little Red Book*, "The woods are full of long drivers" (Penick, 1992, p. 29). The golfer who takes the more cerebral approach to the game and plays for position will be more consistent and better able to avoid an abundance of double and triple bogies (big numbers), thus having a lower overall score.

Simply put, playing position golf is playing to avoid trouble. It is leaving yourself with a good lie and a clear path to the hole on your next shot. This strategy involves choosing a landing area for your shot which takes into account the distance you want your ball to travel and how far you want the ball to be to the left or right in the fairway. Most golfers tend to forget or ignore the fact that they have 14 clubs in their bag, and that the rules do not prohibit you from using a club other than the driver for your tee shot. Some of this stems, again, from the mentality of wanting to get the most distance possible on your tee shot rather than trying to hit your tee shot in the best landing area. If there is a fairway bunker that you cannot easily clear, multiple bunkers that leave you with a small landing area, or simply a narrow fairway, be mindful that teeing off with a fairway wood or a long iron may put you in a better position for your next shot. It is better to have a long-iron or middle-iron shot to the green than a second shot from a fairway bunker or the woods, or a penalty for a lost ball or a ball that is out of bounds.

By getting your ball safely off the tee and in good position in the fairway, you can begin to plan your approach shot as you walk up the fairway to your ball. Club selection on your approach shot is more critical than it was on your tee shot, except on a par-3 hole where the tee shot is itself an approach shot. When hitting into the green you must take into account that the greens are normally guarded by hazards (including water and sand or grass bunkers), and that your shot needs to land as close as possible to the pin in order to avoid finding yourself in 3-putt range.

Your first consideration should be the length of the shot. Today, most courses have markers in or next to the fairway that indicate the ground distance to the center of the green, and these markers are generally placed at 150 yards. If you know which club you consistently hit 150 yards, you can walk off the yardage between the marker and your ball to get a good idea of the club you should use. As you are making your club selection, do not forget to take into consideration the type of lie you have, the weather, and the course conditions.

Above all, make certain that you choose "enough" club to get the ball to the flagstick. Would you be happier with a 6-iron that is 10 feet past the hole, or a 7-iron that is 30 feet short of the hole? Forget about that "career" 7-iron that you hit 155 yards two years ago, and the fact that one of your playing partners is using an 8-iron from the same distance. Most beginning and intermediate-skilled golfers invariably hit the ball short of the pin placement. Tell yourself that the green conditions for good putting will be where there has been less traffic—in most cases, plan to hit past the pin. You should select the club that will get your ball as close to the hole as possible based on the day's conditions and the average length that you are currently hitting each of your clubs, not how you hit last month or last year. Stay in the present, and play each shot based on the circumstances as they currently exist. Also, consider that most holes are designed so that much of the trouble is in front of and to the sides of the green; therefore, if your shot is short of the green or off-line, your next shot could be from trouble.

If your tee shot inadvertently finds trouble, consider your options. Play the shot that affords you the best chance of getting out of trouble and back into play in the fewest strokes possible. Admittedly, no one likes to hit a ball 30 yards sideways; but if that is the best shot you have, play it. The temptation to attempt to hit out through the trees, under some branches, and gain 50 yards over the option of the shot to the side can be overpowering. Before you try this shot, however, consider that hitting one or more of those trees might result in further damage, such as an unplayable lie or the need to take two or more shots to get out of the trees. This can be a very sobering, if not exasperating, experience.

Around the green, your game plan must shift from strokes that require a full swing to those that require less than a full swing—a finesse shot—requiring "good touch." Regardless of whether your approach shot landed on the green or in trouble, the object now is to get the ball into the cup in two strokes—to get "up and down." If your ball is not on the green, the best rule to follow for club selection is to "minimize air time and maximize ground time" as was suggested in Chapter 6 on the short game. In other words, choose a club that will keep the ball in the air for only a short distance, allowing the ball to land on the fringe or on the edge of the green itself and roll the rest of the way toward the hole. This type of shot is more consistent and more predictable than one where a lofted club is used to land and stop the ball close to the hole. A lofted shot requires more exact contact with the ball and a more accurate assessment of the softness and speed of the green. If your approach shot did find the green, try to get your first putt rolling on line and with enough speed so that if you miss it will go 12 to 18 inches past the cup. Your goal, when making that first long putt or when chipping from near the green, should be to get the ball within a three-foot radius of the cup so that you will have a reasonable chance of making your next putt.

Golf, by its very nature, presents many distractions during the play of an 18-hole round. The beauty of the natural surroundings, socializing with friends, the weather conditions, and the many obstacles and hazards that confront you—all work against any effort on your part to maintain the concentration that is necessary to put together a successful round. That is why it is important for you to spend those few extra minutes prior to beginning play to devise a plan for playing each hole so that you will have something to fall back on and to help refocus your attention as the round progresses.

Control of Your Swing

The importance of the mental aspect of golf should be very obvious after reading the previous section on control of your game, yet its importance in the control of your swing is vastly overlooked. The average golfer expends little if any positive mental energy, outside of club selection, when preparing for a shot. A good deal of negative energy is spent, however, in focusing on the desire to avoid water hazards, out-of-bounds, trees, sand bunkers, etc., or on not repeating the disastrously topped, sliced, or fat shot that preceded the current shot. This approach to swinging a golf club will only lead to one calamity after another, making the game a source of stress rather than a source of enjoyment. By putting more emphasis on the mental preparation for a shot, especially on positive swing thoughts, most of your errors can be avoided, thereby reducing stress and increasing your enjoyment of the game.

To assist you in meeting this goal, it is helpful to first consider the golf swing as a three-part process. This text has divided the swing into two parts: the pre-swing fundamentals of grip, alignment, and set-up (Chapter 3) and the swing fundamentals of backswing and forward swing (Chapter 4). Let's now add a third part to this process, the pre-shot routine. The pre-shot routine and the pre-swing fundamentals are mental (cognitive) processes, while the swing phase is a physical process. The success of your golf shot depends much more on the two mental aspects of the shot than on the actual shot execution itself.

The first task you are faced with, the pre-shot routine, occurs before you even have a club in your hands, and its importance dictates that you spend much more time on the decisions related to it than the average golfer is willing to do. "...A sound pre-shot routine is a series of physical and psychological steps taken by a golfer to prepare to hit the best possible shot of which he is capable (Coop, 1993, p. 58). The age-old adage of "failure to plan is planning to fail" is very apropos here. Most of the decision-making process should occur as you approach your ball. If you are walking, rather than riding, you will be able to pace off the distance from the nearest yardage marker to the ball to assist you in the best club selection. You will also be able to judge weather conditions such as wind speed and direction, and playing conditions such as the softness or firmness of the fairway and the greens. Other factors to consider are influenced by a realistic assessment of your abilities and the wisdom of playing percentage golf which favors aiming for targets in the fairway or on the green depending on these abilities. Once you have taken all of these factors into consideration, you can make a more intelligent decision on club selection rather than choosing a club just because it is your favorite club, or because someone in your foursome used the same club from about that same distance.

Now that you have a realistic target in mind and have chosen the appropriate club, you can begin the crucial phase of your pre-shot routine. This routine should consist of several parts which occur in a specific sequence on every shot you play in order to develop consistency, retain confidence, and to help make your swing more repeatable, even during pressure situations. Every time you go to the practice tee, you should work on your pre-shot routine, making it so ingrained that when you are playing, it becomes an automatic part of each shot played. This pre-shot routine process then becomes a "mental safety net," a protected place you have mentally been many times before—during practice and during play. It feels comfortable—somewhat like in a cocoon—and your ability to focus on the shot at hand is dramatically improved.

Here are a few suggestions in regard to this phase of your pre-shot routine. Start at a point about two to four paces directly behind your ball and in line with your intended target. With your club in your hands, pick out a target area in the fairway or on the green, visualize the shot that you would like to produce (possibly a draw or a fade), and "see" that shot land dead center in your intended target area. As you visualize the shot, you should be aware of hazards or obstacles, but focus only on positive swing thoughts and a mental image of your shot floating in and landing softly in your target area. Next, draw an imaginary line back from your target to your ball and pick out an intermediate target a few inches to two feet in front of your ball. With your intermediate target in focus, step off the distance between yourself and your ball and begin the process of establishing your grip, alignment, and set-up as described in the pre-swing fundamentals (Chapter 3). You essentially have two choices to make in respect to the order of events. One is to grip the club correctly at a point away from the ball, then assume your stance around the target line you previously established. The other choice is to sole the club at right angles to that target line you visualized, and then assume your stance around that point. Either way works, although the second one is probably more commonly practiced and makes it easier to align yourself correctly with your target. What is of prime importance here is that you do, indeed, practice a pre-shot routine. If you have prepared yourself correctly for the shot (correct club, positive swing thoughts, and the proper grip, alignment, and set-up) your chances of executing the shot successfully will be much higher than those of the person who is focused on negative thoughts and just haphazardly steps up to the ball and swings, hoping for the best.

The third and final aspect of the swing—the shot execution—constitutes the physical phase of the swing. As the actual shot execution takes less than two seconds, with the downswing taking less than one second, your swing thoughts should be right-brain oriented versus left-brain oriented. Thoughts that are right-brain oriented look at the swing as a whole, seeing a swing that flows with good tempo and balance, and producing the shot that you visualized in your pre-shot routine. These right-brain thoughts "let the swing happen," while left-brain thoughts tend to inhibit your swing by being too analytical. These left-brain thoughts break your swing down into its many parts, thus causing "paralysis from analysis," as we talked about earlier.

There is a great deal of wisdom in Harvey Penick's advice to "Take dead aim" (1992, p. 45). You worked hard at the practice range where you used left-brain thoughts to analyze and correct flaws in your swing . That was a time when you were process-oriented, working on one particular part of your swing. On the course, however, you should be product-oriented, focusing on what the shot looks and feels like, and where it lands. If you made the proper decisions in the pre-shot and pre-swing phases, the shot execution is merely a matter of relaxing and thinking only of good tempo and swinging back and through toward your target.

Control of your swing must include all three phases—the pre-shot routine, the pre-swing, and the shot execution. Too often, golfers will put little or no emphasis on the cognitive aspects of the swing, and then heap all of the blame on the physical aspect of shot execution. The fallacy of this thought process is best summarized by Toski et al.,(1984, p. 261), who state that "…we see in most of our students, and in ourselves as well,…90 percent of the mistakes made playing golf are in those first two mental categories, thus causing faulty swings. Only 10 percent of your mistakes come after you have done everything else correctly and then, because you are human and not a robot, make a bad mechanical swing."

You are going to make mistakes, we all do. There may have been a chemical imbalance in some muscle, or group of muscles and…"stuff" happens! But the number of errors you make can be greatly reduced by taking a little more time before each shot to make intelligent "before" swing decisions.

Control of Yourself

The third and final phase of your game, control of yourself, is one that for some golfers is the most difficult phase and demands the most work. For these people, golf, like the rest of their lives, is a win-or-lose, all-or-none proposition. With the proper attitude and some work, you can keep yourself and your game under control—which will actually improve your scores as well as enhance your enjoyment of the game. Remember, golf is intended to be enjoyed, not endured. Neither your self-esteem nor your life hinge on your golfing abilities. You will do well to keep those thoughts in focus when you hit your drive in the water on number 10 or miss that two-footer on the last hole. Try to relax and enjoy being alive and being there; the sun will come out tomorrow, and your dog will still love you regardless of how many poor shots you hit!

To maximize your potential, you must work on controlling your attitude and your emotions before, during, and after each round of golf or trip to the practice range. Working on your attitude and emotions before the round is the one way to ensure that you will have control over them during the round. If you wait until the round starts, you may hit a couple of bad shots on the first hole or play poorly during the first few holes, thus losing control of yourself before you have a chance to consciously gain control of yourself. As mentioned earlier, it is always a good idea to get to the course early in order to relax and calm your emotions, but it's especially necessary after a tough day at home, work, or on the commute to the course. You want to develop an attitude that is centered on positive swing thoughts. During the round of golf, maintaining control of yourself is a constant battle that becomes easier with practice, and is aided by maintaining a realistic view of your abilities and by keeping the game (with the emphasis on *game*) in the proper perspective. Remember, you play to have fun!

When you have a realistic view of your abilities, it helps you to avoid the pitfall of comparing your abilities with those of your playing partners. When you begin to compare your game with someone else's, you lose control of your game by trying to play his or her type of game, which may not suit your abilities. The best example of this is when you are playing with someone who can hit the ball a long distance. By getting into a long-drive contest with your opponent you will begin to ruin your tempo and feel for the shot, resulting in a rushed, ill-timed swing that produces far more mis-hits and mis-directed shots than home runs. If your swing naturally produces long shots, fine; but try to keep your focus on your target and on maintaining good tempo, rather than on how far you can hit the ball.

On the other hand, if your natural swing produces drives that are shorter than those of your opponents, do not be too disheartened. While everyone would like to experience that exhilarating feeling that comes with hitting a booming 300-yard drive, it is not within the physical capabilities of most golfers to produce such shots. Fortunately, however, 300-yard drives are not necessary to be successful at golf. Keep in mind the fact that the person who gets the ball into the cup in the fewest strokes wins. If you could have a choice between the ability to hit 300-yard drives and the gift of "touch" that is necessary for a good short game, the intelligent golfer would choose the latter. If you feel discouraged when your friends' drives carry 20 yards past where your drives stop, think of the discouragement that they feel when you knock your approach shots stiff to the pin or get up and down from the sand in two shots, consistently beating them with your short game. Be smart, play smart; play to your strengths, not those of others.

Another aspect of your attitude that needs constant attention concerns how you deal with your real opponent, the golf course. As you prepare for a shot, try to form a clear and positive image of how you want your shot to look and of the target area where you want the ball to land. With this positive image of the shot and your target clearly in focus, simply set up to the ball and think only of good tempo and your target. Avoid at all costs any negative thoughts about the results of a poorly executed shot, lest they become a self-fulfilling prophecy. Around water hazards, refrain from setting yourself up for disaster by using a "water ball."

Negative thoughts also create unnecessary tension, which stops your muscles from working in synchrony and causes mental lapses that prevent you from maintaining your concentration until the ball is on its way to the target. Once you have hit the shot, it is over—and nothing can change it. Do not allow a bad shot to ruin your round; instead, learn from the shot, and try to avoid the mistake the next time. If you feel yourself getting flustered after a bad shot, attempt to focus on positive thoughts; walk more slowly to avoid speeding up your pace and ruining the remainder of the round.

At the same time, if the shot was perfect, resist getting too elated, which can also disrupt your tempo and concentration. Be cautious of the euphoria that follows a birdie or an eagle, which might affect your concentration on the next hole, resulting in a bogey or worse. Remember, the round consists of 18 holes, not one hole or one shot, so do not get either down on yourself or too excited. An even tempo and temperate emotional state will aid in maintaining control of yourself and your game.

The final phase of controlling yourself begins after the round is over. During the round, it is easy to get caught up in the frustrations of a bad hole or a couple of poorly executed shots, which may cause you to define the round based on those few down moments. At some point after completing your round, sit down and objectively evaluate it, looking at its strong and weak points. In most instances, you will discover that the strong points far outweigh the weak points, which may help to soothe a bruised ego. In analyzing the round, if you observe a pattern of poor shots in a certain area of your game, it will pinpoint a weakness that you can concentrate on during your next practice session. By noting your strengths and working more on your weaknesses, you can build confidence and develop a more realistic view of your game, which will help you to develop a better game plan to lower your scores in the future.

11 Etiquette, Rules, and Scoring

Etiquette—Keeping Play Safe, Quick, and Courteous

Although not a part of the official rules of golf, etiquette is an unwritten aspect of the game that is intended to make play, in the words of Chuck Hogan (1993), safe, quick and courteous. Many golfers, when they are first learning the game, are hesitant to go out on the course because they are very self conscious and feel that more experienced golfers will not want to play with them if they cannot hit the ball very well and have a high score. In reality, more experienced golfers do not expect a beginner to play that well and are not so concerned with how well a beginner hits the ball as they are with the pace of play. The use of common sense, and understanding and applying the etiquette of the game keeps play safe, allows play to move at a good pace, and makes players more thoughtful of (courteous toward) other golfers and the golf course. More experienced golfers do not expect a beginner always to hit good shots, but they do expect them to have good manners. Hogan (1993) even suggests that a good foundation for learning golf etiquette would be to read Robert Fulghum's book, *All I Really Need to Know I Learned in Kindergarten*. The remaining points of etiquette will be acquired over time from other golfers.

Safely

1. Playing safely means taking the safety of yourself, your playing partners, and other golfers into consideration as you play and practice.
2. Do not attempt to hit a shot until the golfers playing in front of you have moved safely out of your range.
3. If your shot looks like it will hit another golfer or land close to them, yell "Fore!" This is the traditional warning cry in golf to

alert golfers to the danger of an errant shot. If you hear someone yell "fore", turn your back to the direction the warning came from and cover your head until you are certain that the ball has landed.

4. Be careful when walking near another golfer, especially if walking behind them to avoid the potential of being hit by a backswing or follow-through.

5. When swinging a golf club, be aware of the area adjacent to you and of other golfers who may be standing too close to you.

6. When swinging a golf club, be sure to swing in a direction away from others to avoid potential disaster should the club slip out of your hands, the clubhead break on contact with the ground, or you hit someone with dirt and grass from your divot.

7. If you are trying to speed up play by playing "ready golf" (see glossary), be careful when walking ahead of others in your group. Always walk well to the side of the target line of other players and keep an eye out for a misdirected shot.

8. If you should accidentally hit your shot into an adjacent fairway, allow the players on that hole to hit first before you proceed out into that fairway to play your shot.

9. Control your emotions. Avoid yelling or profanity that may disturb golfers nearby. Avoid throwing clubs or other objects that may endanger other golfers.

10. When riding in a golf cart, keep your hands, feet and other body parts inside the cart. It is tragic when golfers get seriously injured by a passing object (another cart, tree, etc.) because they casually allowed an arm or leg to hang out of the cart.

Quickly

1. You should be familiar with the basic fundamentals of playing golf and the rules and etiquette of the game before attempting to play.

2. If you are helping someone improve their swing, save instruction for the practice range and/or the putting green. Instruction on the golf course slows play and decreases the enjoyment of the game for everyone.

3. Do not play golf if you do not have your own set of clubs. It takes far too much time for two or more players to share a set of clubs. Most golf courses do not allow players to share clubs.

4. Slow play takes away some of the enjoyment of the game for everyone. Many courses have marshals who are responsible for keeping play safe and moving at a reasonable pace. Many courses also have set time limits requiring foursomes to complete play in a reasonable time period.

5. Play "ready golf" whenever possible. The player who is ready to hit first plays regardless of who is farthest from the hole. Keep safety in mind. See number 7 above.

6. Think ahead! There are many golfers sharing the golf course. If everyone thinks one or two steps ahead it helps keep play moving more quickly, increasing the enjoyment of the game for everyone.

7. Plan and prepare for your next shot as you approach your ball while the other players in your group are hitting their shots. This also helps in your own course management, as discussed earlier. When it is your turn, proceed quickly and limit yourself to one practice swing.

8. Watch where your ball lands and rolls, using a landmark to help mark the last spot that you saw it if it disappears from view. Helping the others in your group watch where their shots end up makes it easier to locate their ball and keep play moving.

9. If your group is unable to keep pace with the group in front (if there is an open hole between your group and the group in front) allow the group behind you to "play through." This is done most efficiently on a par-3 hole. When the group reaches the tee have your group step off the green and allow them to hit their tee shots. As the group behind is walking to the green someone in your group can putt. When the group behind reaches the green, allow them to finish the hole and play through.

10. If you and your playing partners are using the full five minutes allotted to look for a lost ball (you should not do this unless you are in a tournament), and you are holding up the players behind you, allow them to play through.

11. If you are riding in a golf cart and are not allowed to take the cart off the cart path, be sure to take several clubs along with you to avoid having to return to your cart. Work with your riding part-

ner so that one of you drives the cart forward after each shot. If necessary, the person with the cart should carry clubs to the other player upon reaching the green. Park the cart next to or behind the green so that you can quickly drive to the next tee.

12. As you approach the putting green, survey the position of your ball so that you will have a good estimate of the distance to the hole, the amount of break and the speed of the putt. While someone else in your group is putting you can be lining up your putt as long as you do not interfere with their play (Figure 11.1).

13. The person whose ball is closest to the hole should tend the pin, if necessary, for the other players. The player who finishes the hole first should take responsibility for tending the pin and replacing the pin after the last player completes the hole.

14. Move off of the green quickly, checking to be sure that you do not leave any clubs or personal items, and proceed to the next tee. You can discuss and record your scores on the way to the next tee.

15. When you first start playing golf you will struggle with your swing and the distance and direction of your shots. Don't worry; golf is just a game. Do not be concerned with your score or how well you hit the ball. If it makes the game easier and helps speed up play, tee the ball up on shots from the tee and the fairway. Don't hit shots from the bunker. Retrieve the ball from the bunker, rake your footprints and drop the ball next to the bunker. Play by the 5 and 5 rule, or some variation of the rule.

The 5 and 5 rule says that you make 5 swings at the ball whether you hit it or not, and if the ball is not on the green, pick it up and follow the rest of your group until you get about 10 yards

Fig. 11.1. Plan and line up your putt while another player is putting.

from the green. Drop the ball and make 5 more swings. If the ball is not in the hole, pick it up and record a 10 for your score. If you have made 10 swings, that is enough on any hole and you will not hold up the pace of play for your group. As your skill level improves, you can modify this to become the 4 and 4 rule, and so on.

Courteously

Courtesy to Other Players

1. Play in the proper order from the tee. The order of play is determined by lot on the first hole. Beginning with the second hole, the player with "honors" (the player with the lowest score on the previous hole) should be allowed to hit first. If more than one player has the same score on a hole, the order of play remains the same.

2. Try to refrain from talking or making excessive movements (especially in another player's line of vision) while a shot is being played (Figure 11.2). "Fore" is sometimes used to request that talking and movement cease so that a shot can be played without disruption.

Fig. 11.2. Avoid excessive noise and movement while another player is playing a shot.

3. Keep noise levels (loud talking, yelling, the sound of cart motors, etc.) down. The enjoyment of making a nice shot or a difficult putt may be shared with the players in your group, but without disturbing other players on the course who may be attempting a shot at the same time.

4. Along with the joy of making a nice shot comes the frustration of hitting a poor shot or getting a bad break. Keep in mind that golf is just a game, and make an effort to keep your frustrations under control. Brooding, moody behavior, offensive language and throwing clubs are all examples of inappropriate behavior on the golf course. Any of these behaviors diminish the en-

Fig. 11.3. Do not step on the line of another players putt.

Fig. 11.4. Watch your shadow so that it does not interfere with another putt.

Fig. 11.5. Move your ball marker if it interferes with another player's putt.

Fig. 11.6. Replace your divots.

joyment of the game for you and your playing companions. Repeated occurrences of this type of behavior may make it difficult to find other golfers who are willing to play with you.

5. Be careful when walking on the putting green so that you do not step on the line of another player's putt (Figure 11.3).

6. While tending the pin, be careful not to step on anyone's line. Also, watch your shadow so that is does not interfere with another player's putt (Figure 11.4).

7. Mark and lift your ball if it is on another player's line. If your ball marker will interfere with that player's putt, move it one or more clubhead lengths to the side (Figure 11.5). Note a permanent object to use as a reference so that when it is your turn to putt you can replace your ball marker in its original position.

Courtesy to the Course

1. Leave the course in better condition than you found it.

2. Place all litter in a trash container.

3. Try to keep your golf cart on the cart path as much as possible, especially when the course is wet. Keep carts (riding carts and pull carts) well away from the green.

4. Avoid taking several practice swings, especially if taking divots with each one.

5. When you do take a divot, replace it (Figure 11.6) on fescue grass fairways and tamp it down. On Bermuda grass fairways it is not necessary to replace your divot, as the grass will die anyway. Instead, use sand that is provided in the bottle on your cart to fill in the divot hole. Most courses also provide sand at the tee box on par-3 holes to fill in the divot holes from tee shots with irons.

6. When you enter a bunker, enter at the lowest side, taking the shortest route to your ball. En-

tering from the high side pushes the sand down and away from the edge (lip) of the bunker (Figure 11.7). If someone was inconsiderate enough to have left footprints in the bunker, please rake them also. If is very frustrating to find your ball in someone's footprint when the bunker was not raked.

7. Do not place your bag on the green.
8. Repair all ball marks on the green (Figure 11.8)—yours and others you may find.
9. Repair any scuff marks on the green (after you have putted).
10. When removing the pin, place it gently on the green out of the other players' lines.
11. Be careful not to damage the edge (lip) of the cup with the flagstick, your foot or a club. Retrieve your ball from the hole with your hand, not your putter.

Fig. 11.7. *Enter sand bunkers from the low side. Entering from the high side damages the lip of the bunker.*

Rules

Golf is a civil game, and unlike most other games is officiated by the players rather than by umpires or referees. The rules, like handicaps, make play equitable by insuring that everyone is playing the same game. The original 13 rules written in Scotland in 1744 were intended for ladies and gentlemen who would play with honor and integrity. Those 13 rules form the basis for the present 34 rules on which the USGA and the Royal and Ancient Golf Club at St. Andrews have collaborated to make play the same worldwide. It is important to keep in mind that the rules are designed to make play equitable, not to penalize you. Knowing and understanding the rules can help you. For example, if your ball lies in casual water, you may drop it within one club length of the nearest point of relief with no penalty. That is much better than splashing yourself with mud and water and possibly not getting the ball out of the water.

Fig. 11.8. *Repair all ball marks on the green.*

The rules of golf can be quite complicated and often confusing for golfers of all ability levels. We would like to simplify the wording of these rules and summarize them so that understanding them is a less daunting task.

Prior to Beginning Play

1. **Scoring** – there are two types of play: stroke (medal) play and match play.
   a. In **Stroke** (medal) play, the score is determined by the number of strokes a player or team takes for the round(s) of golf. The player/team with the lowest score is the winner.
   b. In **Match** play, the score is determined by the number of holes won rather than by total strokes. The winner is the person or team in the lead by a number of holes greater than the number of holes left to be played. For example, 3 and 2, is the score when a person/team is 3 up with 2 holes to play.
2. **Number of clubs** – under Rule 4-4, a, you may play with a maximum of 14 clubs in your bag. If you have more than 14 clubs in your bag you are penalized for each hole at which the infraction occurred. In stroke play, you are penalized *two strokes per hole*, with a *maximum of 4 strokes*. In match play, the penalty is *loss of hole*, with a *maximum of 2 holes*.
3. **Identifying your ball** – you should place an identifying mark(s) on your ball prior to beginning play so that you will be able to verify that you are playing with the correct ball. The penalty for playing with the wrong ball, under Rules 15-2 and 15-3, is *two strokes* in stroke play and *loss of hole* in match play.

Teeing Ground

1. **Order of play** – Rules 10-1 and 10-2 state that the order of play on the first tee is decided by lot (drawing names, flipping a coin, spinning a tee, etc.), or simply by being courteous and allowing a fellow player the privilege of teeing off first. On each succeeding hole, the score on the previous hole decides the order of play. *Honors* (the privilege of teeing off first), belongs to the person with the lowest previous score. If two players have the same score on the previous hole, the person with honors on that hole retains honors on the next hole.

2. **Tee markers** – when teeing off you must tee your ball within an imaginary rectangle that is formed by an imaginary line between the two tee markers and imaginary lines that extend two club lengths behind the tee markers (Figure 11.9). Failure to do so, under Rule 11-4 a, and b, results in a *two-stroke* penalty in stroke play or *loss of hole* in match play.

3. **Accidentally knocking the ball off of the tee** – if the ball falls off of the tee or you accidentally knock it off as you address it, you may re-tee the ball under Rule 11-3, with *no penalty*.

4. **Whiff** – if you make a swing at the ball and miss (whiff) it, this counts as one stroke.

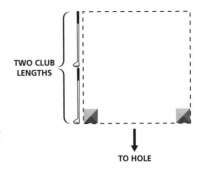

Fig. 11.9. Tee box—formed by the tee markers and imaginary boundary lines.

Ball in Play

1. **Order of play** – after the tee shot, the person farthest from the hole should play first. However, in order to speed up play, you can play "ready golf" where the player who is ready first plays the next shot. If this requires you to walk ahead of the other players in your group, use caution, staying well to the side of those behind you. Also, do not walk ahead of, around or near another player if that will distract them in preparing their shot.

2. **Play the ball as it lies** – if you improve the position or lie of your ball, the area of your intended swing or your line of play by moving, bending, or breaking anything that is growing or fixed, you will, under Rule 13-2, incur a *two-stroke penalty* in stroke play and *loss of hole* in match play.

3. **Lost ball** – if you hit a shot and cannot find your ball within the five-minute time limit, under Rule 27-1, you must return to the spot where you last played your original ball, taking a *stroke and distance* penalty.

4. **Out-of-bounds** – if you hit a shot and you find that it is out-of-bounds you must, under Rule 27-1, return to the spot where you last played your original ball and take a *stroke and distance* penalty. The ball is considered to be out-of-bounds when the *entire* ball is outside the stakes, fence or line that defines out-of-bounds (Figure 11.10).

Fig. 11.10. The ball is out-of-bounds when the entire ball is outside the stakes, fence or line which defines out-of-bounds.

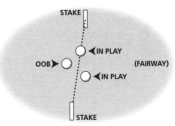

Fig. 11.11. Unplayable lie.

Fig. 11.12. Loose impediments.

Fig. 11.13. Obstructions, moveable and immovable.

5. **Provisional ball** – you can save time, and a long walk, if you play a provisional ball when you believe that your ball may be lost or out-of-bounds. When playing a provisional ball, you must first inform your fellow players that you intend to play a provisional ball. If your original ball is not lost or out-of-bounds you can pick up your provisional ball and play your original ball with *no penalty*.

6. **Unplayable lie** – you may declare your ball unplayable anywhere on the course except in a hazard. If your ball is in a position from which you cannot play your next shot (Figure 11.11) you may, under Rule 28:

   a. Take a *stroke and distance* penalty and play another ball from where you last played your original ball;

   b. Drop your ball taking a *one-stroke* penalty,

      i. Within two club-lengths of the spot where the ball lays, but not nearer the hole, or

      ii. Anywhere behind the spot where the ball lays along an imaginary line that runs from the hole through that spot.

7. **Loose impediments** (naturally occurring objects such as stones, twigs, leaves, etc. that are not solidly imbedded or growing) – you are allowed, under Rule 23-1, to remove loose impediments (Figure 11.12) that interfere with your swing or stance anywhere through the green (see glossary) with *no penalty*. However, if your ball moves after you touch or move a loose impediment that is within one club length of your ball, you are assessed a penalty of *one stroke*.

8. **Obstructions** (man-made objects such as cart paths, buildings, benches, trash cans, bottles, etc., and are either *movable* or *immovable*) – you may, under Rule 24-1, and 24-2, obtain relief from an obstruction (Figure 11.13) with *no penalty* as follows:

   a. **Movable** – move the obstruction. If the ball moves you must replace it without penalty.

   b. **Immovable** – drop your ball within one club length of the nearest point of relief, but no closer to the hole.

9. **Casual water, ground under repair, hole made by a burrowing animal** – you may, under Rule 25-1, obtain relief from any of these abnormal ground conditions with *no penalty* if they interfere with your swing or your stance (Figure 11.14). If there is reasonable evidence that your ball was lost in one of these abnormal

ground conditions you may drop another ball within one club length from where the ball entered the condition, but no nearer the hole, with *no penalty*.

10. **Hazards** (sand and water) – if your ball lies in a hazard you may not a) test the surface of the hazard, b) touch the ground or water in the hazard with your club prior to making your swing, or c) touch or move loose impediments in the hazard. If you do any of the above you will, under Rule 13-4 a, b, and c, incur a penalty of *two strokes* in stroke play and *loss of hole* in match play.

Fig. 11.14. Casual water.

a. **Sand bunker** – you must play your ball as it lies in the bunker or declare the ball unplayable and proceed under Rule 28 (see number 6, above).

b. **Regular water hazard** – if your ball enters a regular water hazard (marked by *yellow* lines or stakes) you may, under Rule 26-1 a, and b:

  i. Play the ball as it lies,

  ii. Take a *stroke and distance* penalty, or

  iii. Drop the ball any distance behind the water hazard along an imaginary line that extends from the hole through the spot where the ball entered the hazard, under a penalty of *one stroke* (Figure 11.15).

c. **Lateral water hazard** – if your ball enters a lateral water hazard (marked by red lines or stakes) you may, under Rule 26-1 a, b, and c:

  i. Play the ball as it lies,

  ii. Take a *stroke and distance* penalty,

  iii. Drop a ball any distance behind the hazard along an imaginary line that extends from the hole through the spot where the ball entered the hazard, under penalty of *one stroke*, or

  iv. Drop a ball within two club lengths of the point where the ball crossed the margin of the hazard, on either side of the hazard, but not nearer the hole, under penalty of *one stroke* (Figure 11.16).

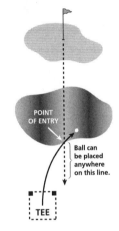

Fig. 11.15. Dropping from a regular water hazard.

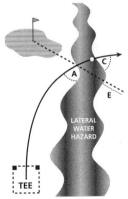

Fig. 11.16. Dropping from a lateral water hazard. Ball may be dropped anywhere along line E or in zone A or C.

On the Putting Green

1. **Ball marks and spike marks** – as mentioned in the section on etiquette, you should repair all ball marks and spike marks on the green, yours and those left by others. Ball marks may be repaired anywhere on the green with *no penalty*. When spike marks or scuff marks are in the line of your putt you may not repair them until after you putt. If you repair these marks that are in the line of your putt *prior* to putting, you will, under Rule 16-1, incur a penalty of *two strokes* in stroke play and *loss of hole* in match play.

2. **Hitting another player's ball** – if you make a stroke while your ball is on the putting green and it strikes another players ball, which is also on the green (Figure 11.17), under Rule 19-5 a, you incur a penalty of *two strokes* in stroke play, but there is *no penalty* in match play. However, the other player must replace their ball as close as possible to its original spot on the green.

Fig. 11.17. Hitting another player's ball when your ball is on the green.

Penalties

Two-Stroke Penalties

1. Carrying more than 14 clubs in your bag.
2. Playing the wrong ball.
3. Teeing the ball outside the imaginary boundaries on the tee box that are formed by the tee markers and a two club-length distance behind the tee markers.
4. Improving your lie.
5. Grounding your club in a hazard, or testing the surface of the hazard.
6. Repairing spike marks on the line of your putt.
7. Hitting another player's ball when you are both on the putting green.
8. Hitting the flagstick when your ball is on the putting green.

Fig. 11.18. Hitting the flagstick when your ball is on the green is a two stroke penalty.

One-Stroke Penalties

1. Taking relief from an unplayable lie.
2. Having your ball move when you move a *loose impediment* within one club length of your ball.

3. Taking relief from a regular water hazard or lateral water hazard.
4. Delaying longer than 10 seconds in tapping your ball in when it is overhanging the lip of the hole.

No Penalty

1. Whiffing (missing) the ball when you make a swing. The swing is counted as a stroke, but there is no penalty.
2. Accidentally knocking your ball off of the tee before your swing.
3. Picking up your provisional ball, providing that your original ball is found, or is not out-of-bounds.
4. Removing a *moveable obstruction*. If your ball moves you can replace it with no penalty.
5. Removing a loose impediment anywhere through the green, provided that your ball does not move.
6. Taking relief from casual water, ground under repair or a hole made by a burrowing animal.

Scoring

The scorecard (Figure 11.20) is your road map to the golf course. It is filled with helpful information concerning yardage, the par and handicap of each hole, course ratings and slope ratings, the location of out-of-bounds, local rules and a diagram of each hole. All of this information is especially helpful when playing a course for the first time. For example, knowledge of the length of each hole is useful in club selection, particularly on par-3 holes, and the diagrams of each hole may show hazards (sand and water) that you will want to avoid. Making full use of the information printed on the scorecard can help you to take advantage of the course's weaknesses and your strengths to shoot a lower score and enjoy the round more.

Golf courses vary in length from approximately 5,500 to over 7,000 yards for men, and from 5,000 to 6,000 yards for women. How long the course will play depends on which set of tees you choose to play. Traditionally, courses are longest from the black (championship) tees, which are for highly skilled amateur and professional golfers. The majority of men play from the blue (regular men's) tees, while beginners and seniors usually play from the white (front men's) tees. Some courses have green or gold tees for senior golfers. Women generally play from the red (ladies') tees. Today, many courses no longer label or designate specific sets of tees as ladies, seniors, championship, etc. Instead, they simply list the color of the different tees, and the corresponding length of the course from each set of tees. You should feel free to choose the set of tees you want to play based on your skill level, rather than age or gender. Individual holes range in length from just under 100 to over 600 yards. The par for each hole includes one, two or three strokes to get on the green (depending on the length of the hole), plus two putts.

USGA Yardage for Par

Fig. 11.19. USGA yardage for determining par for a hole.

Par	Ladies	Gentlemen
3	≤ 210	≤ 250
4	211 – 400	251 – 470
5	401 – 575	≥ = 471
6	≥ = 576	

Your score on each hole has a number and a name based on its relation to par. A hole in one is usually called an *ace*. A score of two under par (e.g., three on a par-5 hole) is referred to as an *eagle*. One stroke under par is a *birdie*, one stroke over par is a *bogey*, and two or more strokes over par is a double bogey, triple bogey, etc. *Par* is the standard of excellence that represents the score that an expert golfer should make on a particular hole, based on the length and difficulty of the hole.

Unless you consider yourself to be an expert (less than eight percent of all golfers can break 80 on a regular basis), you would be wise, in the beginning, to take Hogan's (1993) advice and "change 'par' to something that makes sense." If you expect to make par on every hole you are setting yourself up for failure before you hit your first shot. "Par" can be any score you want it to be. If your best score ever on the 9th hole at your course is a 6, make 6 "your par" for the that hole, regardless of the par listed on the scorecard. If you want to measure how well you are playing, "do so by the amount of fun you're having, not by a number" (Hogan, 1993). Golf is a game; not work, it should be *fun*!

Handicaps

How to Establish a Handicap

The use of a handicap is a method of equalizing competition among players. Your handicap is calculated when your club professional turns

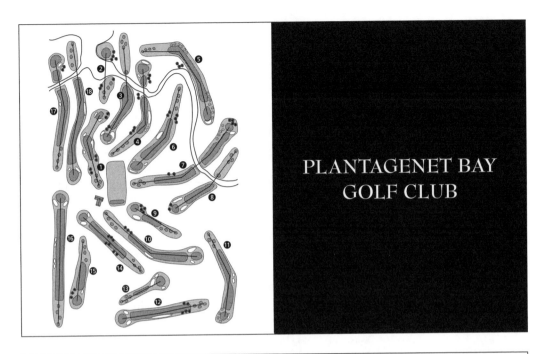

PLANTAGENET BAY
GOLF CLUB

HOLE	1	2	3	4	5	6	7	8	9	OUT	10	11	12	13	14	15	16	17	18	IN	TOTAL	HCP	NET	INITIAL
BLACK	371	201	418	424	501	440	520	408	198	3481	415	440	377	201	380	215	545	375	560	3508	6989			
BLUE	341	190	403	410	480	428	502	395	183	3332	398	418	360	185	362	185	515	360	538	3321	6653			
WHITE	328	182	375	388	458	397	488	381	170	3167	382	402	345	171	345	170	489	340	522	3166	6333			
RED	280	158	358	363	440	380	467	365	161	2972	356	378	325	150	330	154	463	326	501	2983	5955			
PAR	4	3	4	4	5	4	5	4	3	36	4	4	4	3	4	3	5	4	5	36	72			
HANDICAP	11	3	13	1	7	9	5	15	17		12	8	18	4	14	6	16	2	10					
SCORER:							ATTEST:											DATE:					

Course Rating/Slope: Black 72.1/133   Blue 71.3/131   White 69.8/125   Red 68.7/124

Play is governed by USGA Rules. Please replace divots, rake bunkers, and repair ball marks. Allow faster groups to play through.

Fig. 11.20. Scorecard.

your scores into the USGA, or enters them into a USGA computer link at the golf shop. Each of your scores is then subtracted from the course rating (located on the scorecard) for the set of tees and golf course that you played. The course rating is the difficulty rating that the USGA has assigned to each golf course and each set of tees on the course. The difference between your score and the course rating is called a handicap differential. The computer takes the 10 best (lowest) handicap differentials from your last 20 scores. The 10 best handicap differentials are averaged. This average is then multiplied by .96 to obtain your individual handicap. Professional golfers normally have a handicap of +4 or better. Top amateurs will often play to a handicap of between 2 and 0 (scratch), while beginners might have a handicap closer to 30.

In the late 1980s, the USGA instituted the use of slope ratings so that your handicap would "travel" better when you visited other locations. By using the slope rating system, if the golf course that you are visiting is more difficult than your "home" course, you will have a higher handicap at that course, and vice versa. The slope rating system also makes handicaps more valid. Prior to this system, two golfers might have the same handicap even though they established their handicap on different courses that might have different levels of difficulty. When these golfers with equal handicaps played each other they were not always equal. Also, your handicap stayed the same even if you played from a more difficult or an easier set of tees at your own course.

How to Use Your Handicap

Stroke (Medal) Play

In competition, your handicap is used for both stroke (medal) and match play. In stroke play, you simply subtract your handicap from your gross score. The player with the lowest net score for the match or tournament is the winner. For example, if you have a handicap of 14 and you shoot an 86 in the first round, you would have a net score of 72 (86 − 14 = 72). Simple.

Match Play

Match play is scored by holes won rather than by total strokes. The winner is the person or team in the lead by a number of holes greater than the number of holes left to be played. For example, 3 and 2 is the score when a player or team is 3 up with 2 holes to play. If the match is tied at the end of the round, the match goes to sudden death. In sudden death, the first player or team to win a hole wins the match. To use your handicap, start by subtracting your handicap from your opponent's handicap. If you have a handicap of 6 and your opponent has a handicap of 12, there is a difference of 6. Since you are the better golfer (you have a lower handicap), you would give your opponent 1 stroke on the 6 hardest holes. How do you know which are the 6 hardest holes? Look at your scorecard, and find the line with the heading—Handicap. This column lists the handicap for each hole. The most difficult hole is the number 1 handicap (hole number 4), the least difficult hole is the number 18 handicap (hole number 12), and all of the other holes fall in between these two. Since you must give your opponent 1 stroke on the 6 hardest holes, you will give these strokes on holes 4, 17, 2, 13, 7 and 15. Note that all of the odd numbered handicapped holes are on the front and all of the even numbered handicapped holes are on the back. This is done so that all of the hardest holes are spaced out. If the hardest holes happened to be the last six holes you might close the match out before your opponent got to use their handicap strokes.

From the Tee to the Green

The objective in golf is very simple—advance a small (1.68 inch diameter) ball into a 4.25-inch cup that is sunk into the putting green in the fewest strokes possible over 18 holes. If you have never played the game before, you will want to know where to begin, how to proceed and which clubs to use in different situations. This section will provide the beginner with a basic answer to some of these types of questions.

The Tee Shot

The fun begins at the tee box (Figure 11.21, A), which has closely mown grass and tee markers (Figure 11.21, B) to indicate where you can tee your ball for the first shot on each hole. You are allowed to "tee up" the ball on a wooden or plastic tee anywhere in an imaginary rectangle formed by the two tee markers, and an area of up to two club lengths behind the markers. In deciding which club to use for your tee shot you should consult your scorecard. First, determine the length of the hole (this is especially important on par-3 holes), then check to see if there are any hazards that might come into play. On the par-4 hole depicted

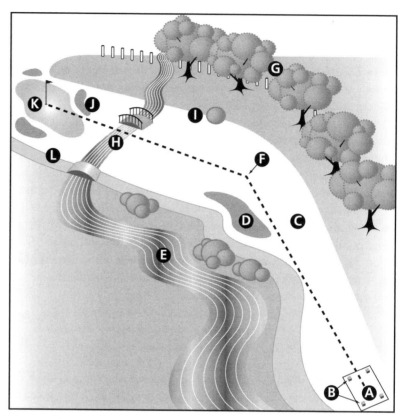

Fig. 11.21. Typical par-4 hole.

A – Tee box
B – Tee markers
C – Fairway
D – Fairway bunker
E – Lateral water hazard
F – Target landing area

G – Out-of-bounds
H – Regular water hazard
I – 150-yard marker
J – Greenside bunkers
K – Flagstick
L – Cart path

in Figure 11.21, you will see trees off to the right side of the fairway (Figure 11.21, C), and a fairway bunker (Figure 11.21, D) guarding the corner of the dogleg. Also, there is a lateral water hazard (Figure 11.21, E), marked by red lines or stakes, to the left of the fairway bunker.

You will want to avoid both a long sand shot from a fairway bunker and hitting your ball into a lateral water hazard (1 stroke penalty). Therefore, you should pick a landing area for your tee shot that is in the right, center of the fairway (Figure 11.20, F). This is a fairly large and open landing area, leaving you with a margin for error in the event that you do not hit a perfect tee shot. Depending on how far you hit your driver, you may want to use your 3-wood to avoid hitting your tee shot through the fairway and into the trees on the far side, possibly resulting in a ball lost or out-of-bounds (Figure 11.21, G). If your ball is lost or out-of-bounds, it would result in a stroke and distance penalty. Because the 3-wood is shorter, and has more loft (imparts less side-spin) than your driver, it is generally a more accurate and predictable club to use in a situation such as this where there is danger on both the left and right sides of the fairway. Remember, the prize goes to the person with the lowest score, not necessarily the person who hits the longest drives.

The Approach Shot

After a nicely struck tee shot to your intended target landing area in the center of the fairway (Figure 11.21, F), you have a clear approach shot to the green. As you are walking up to your ball, start thinking about club selection for your next shot. First check your lie and the conditions surrounding your ball. Is the ball sitting up nicely on the fairway grass, is it in an old divot hole, on the side of a slope, is the wind blowing, etc? Also, walk off the distance from the nearest yardage marker, and check for obstacles and hazards around the green that will influence your club selection. You will notice a large clump of pampas grass (Figure 11.21, I) on the right edge of the fairway that serves as a 150-yard marker on this hole. Most courses use similar types of markers to indicate yardage to the center of the green. Some of these markers are large colored discs in the center of the fairway to mark 200, 150 and 100 yards. Because most courses now have laser range finders, they will mark the tops of fairway sprinkler heads to provide more yardage markers. As your skills improve you should make note of how far you hit each of your clubs so that you can make better use of yardage markers in making club selections for each shot.

Your ball is about 160 yards (about 10 yards short of the 150-yard marker) from the center of the green. Which club should you hit? If you know that you can consistently hit your 7-iron 150 yards (in the air, not carry and roll) you would select one more club for your approach shot. A 6-iron, is ½ inch longer and has about 3-4 degrees less loft than the 7-iron, giving it approximately 10 yards more carry than a 7-iron. Proper club selection will allow you to carry your approach shot over the regular water hazard (Figure 11.21, H), and the greenside bunker

(Figure 11.21, J) that guards the front of the green, and land it close to the flagstick (Figure 11.21, K) in the center of the green. If you are not sure which club to hit, use one more club than you think you need and swing easy. If you are tense or have negative thoughts about the shot you might mishit it, leaving it in the water or sand short of the green. As you approach the green, be careful and keep riding carts on the cart path (Figure 11.21, L) when you are near the green; also keep your bag well away from the green.

When you are playing golf you should expect to hit many bad shots and a few good shots. If you understand that most of your shots will not be as good as you would like it will help you to enjoy the game more, and leave the course wanting to come back tomorrow and try to shoot a lower score. If you expect every shot to be good, and focus on your bad shots, you will make yourself and your companions miserable by the end of the day. We go to our job to work, we go to the golf course to play. Golf is a game; it is supposed to be fun. When you go out to play, please do not forget to play safely, quickly and courteously so that you and everyone else can enjoy this great game even more.

Glossary

Ace–A hole completed in one stroke. A hole-in-one.

Address–The position assumed by a player prior to executing a stroke.

Approach shot–Any full shot that is played with the intention of having the ball finish up on the putting green.

Apron–The grass border around the green which is cut shorter than the fairway, but not as short as the green.

Away–The ball or player whose ball is farthest from the hole. The player whose ball is "away" should play first.

Best ball–A type of competition in which the lower score of partners is counted in the match.

Birdie–A score that is one stroke less than the specified par for a hole.

Bite–Backspin that is imparted to a ball which causes it to stop quickly when it lands on the green.

Bogey–A score that is one stroke more than the specified par for a hole.

Bounce–The distance in degrees that the trailing edge of the sole of the club extends below the leading edge of the clubface.

Break of the green–The slant or slope of a putting green that should be taken into account when deciding how much a putt will curve.

Bunker–A depression that is adjacent to the green, or sometimes out next to the fairway.

Caddy–A person who carries a player's clubs and assists the player as provided by the rules of golf.

Carry–The distance that a ball flies in the air before hitting the ground.

Casual water–Any temporary accumulation of water that is not part of a water hazard.

Chip shot–A short shot that is played from just off the putting green. This shot has a low trajectory that carries for a short distance, then rolls to the hole.

Chunk–A swing where the clubhead contacts the ground before contacting the ball, limiting the distance of the shot. (See also **fat** shot.)

Closed clubface–A clubface that is turned to face left of the intended line of flight for a RH golfer, or to the right for a LH golfer.

Closed stance–An address position where the dominant foot is pulled back slightly away from a line that runs parallel with the intended line of flight. (See **dominant** foot.)

Course rating–A numbered rating that is determined by the USGA, which represents the playing difficulty of a course from the various tee markers.

Cup–The hole on the putting green, or the metal or plastic liner that fits into the hole.

Divot–A piece of the turf that is displaced by the clubhead during the swing.

Dogleg–A left or right curvature of the fairway.

Double bogey–A score that is two strokes more than the specified par for a hole.

Double eagle–A score that is three strokes less than the specified par for a hole.

Down–The number of holes or strokes that a player is behind his opponent; e.g., two-down, three-down, etc.

Draw–A shot that curves gently from right to left for a RH, or from left to right for a LH.

Driver–The one-wood.

Drop–The act of putting the ball into play when taking relief from a hazard, unplayable lie, etc., according to the rules. The player should stand erect, holding the ball at shoulder height and arm's length, and drop the ball.

Dub–A poorly hit shot.

Duck (or snap) hook–A ball that goes radically left for a RH, or radically right for a LH.

Duffer–A poorly skilled player.

Eagle–A score that is two strokes less than the specified par for a hole.

Explosion shot–A shot played from a sand trap where the club contacts the sand behind the ball and sand is displaced from the trap, in a spray, carrying the ball out with it.

Fade–A shot that curves gently from left to right for a RH, or from right to left for a LH.

Fairway -The closely mown grass between the tee and the putting green that is bordered by the rough.

Fat shot–A swing where the clubhead contacts the ground before contacting the ball, limiting the distance of ball flight. (See also **chunk**.)

Flag, flagstick, or pin–The tall fiberglass or metal rod with attached flag that indicates the location of the hole on the putting green.

Flat swing–A swing that is less vertical than normal. At the top of the backswing, the club is below the swing plane that was established at address.

Follow through—The portion of the swing that occurs after contact with the ball.

Fore—A warning shouted to anyone who might be in danger of being hit by your ball. Also used as a request for silence when others are about to hit.

Foursome—A group of four players who may or may not be involved in a match.

Fringe—See **apron**.

Grain—The direction that the grass grows on the green. This plays an important role in determining the speed of the putt and how much the putt will curve.

Green—The smooth, closely cut putting surface that contains the hole.

Gross score—The total number of strokes that it takes a player to complete a round of golf.

Ground under repair (GUR)—Any portion of a hole or of the course that is undergoing repair, and is so indicated by lines or stakes.

Halved—In match play, when two competitors, or teams, take the same number of strokes, thus tying a hole.

Handicap—The number of strokes assigned to a player based on his average scoring ability. A player's handicap allows him to compete equally with other golfers of all ability levels.

Hazard—Technically, bunkers and water hazards, but may include trees or other obstacles.

Hole—One of the 18 distinct sections of a golf course, or the 4 1/4-inch diameter hole that is located on the putting green.

Hole high—A shot that stops even with the hole, but off to one side.

Hole out—To knock the ball into the cup, thus completing play on that hole.

Honor—The right to hit first on the tee shot, as determined by the lowest score on the previous hole, or by a coin toss on the first hole.

Hook—A shot that curves from right to left for a RH, or from left to right for a LH.

LPGA—Ladies Professional Golf Association.

Lateral water hazard—A water hazard, marked by red lines or stakes, that runs parallel to the line of play.

Lie—(1) The position on the ground at which the ball comes to rest at the end of a shot.
(2) The number of strokes the player has taken to reach that point on that hole.

(3) The angle of the shaft of the club in relation the the clubhead; i.e., flat, normal, upright.

Loft–The degree of pitch from vertical that is manufactured into the clubface.

Loose impediments–Natural objects that are not growing, such as rocks, sticks, pine cones, etc.

Match play–A form of competition where each hole is won by the person who takes the least number of strokes on that hole, and the winner of the match is determined by the one who wins the most holes.

Medalist–The player who shoots the lowest qualifying round for a tournament.

Medal play–A form of competition where the winner is determined by the player who takes the least number of total strokes. (See also **stroke play.**)

Mulligan–A second, but illegal, drive taken from the first tee when the first drive was unsatisfactory.

Nassau–A scoring method in a match based on a total of three points, one for the winner of each nine, and one for the winner of the total eighteen holes.

Net score–A player's gross score, minus his handicap.

Obstruction–Any man-made object on the course, either movable, or immovable, with the exception of objects that define boundaries, e.g., stakes, fences, and walls.

Open clubface–A clubface that is turned so that it faces to the right of the intended line of flight for a RH, to the left for a LH.

Open stance–An address position where the target foot is pulled back slightly away from a line that runs parallel with the intended line of flight. (See **target** foot.)

Out-of-Bounds (OOB)–Areas outside the property of the golf course that are marked by white stakes or fences, or as designated on the score card.

PGA–Professional Golfers' Association.

Par–The score representing a standard of excellence, based on the length of the hole, and allowing for two putts.

Penalty stroke–A stroke added to a player's score due to an infraction of the rules.

Pitch shot–A short shot that has a high trajectory and lands on the green with little or no roll.

Provisional ball–A second ball that is played when a player knows, or suspects, that his first ball is lost or out-of-bounds. A player must declare that this is a provisional ball, otherwise it becomes the ball in play with the penalty of stroke and distance.

Pulled shot–A shot that flies on a relatively straight line, but to the left of the target for a RH, and to the right of the target for a LH.

Pushed shot–A shot that flies on a relatively straight line, but to the right of the target for a RH, and to the left of the target for a LH.

Ready golf–In an attempt to speed up play, players' groups (and in agreement among themselves) may play when they are ready – providing it is safe to do so – even though they may not be "away" as defined within the rules of golf.

Rough–The area that borders the fairway and surrounds the tee and green, where the grass and other vegetation is allowed to grow longer than the fairway.

Rub-of-the-green–An incident where a ball that is in motion, or at rest, is stopped or deflected by an outside agency where the results may be favorable or unfavorable.

Sand trap–A depression filled with sand. (See also **bunker**.)

Sand wedge–A specialty iron that is heavier and has a wider sole than the other irons, which makes it easier to hit from a sand trap.

Scratch player–A player with a handicap of zero who normally plays at or near par.

Shank–A shot that usually goes off at a sharp angle right for RH, or left for LH, due to contacting the ball with the hosel (see **Figure 2.1**), rather than the clubface.

Slice–A shot that curves from left to right for a RH, right to left for a LH.

Slope rating–A numbered rating system that was formulated by the USGA that allows players to compete more equally when they have established their handicaps on different courses.

Sole–The bottom of the clubhead, or the act of resting the clubhead on the ground at address.

Square stance–An address position where both feet are on a line that runs parallel to the intended line of flight.

Stance–The set-up or positioning of the feet, body, and arms when addressing the ball.

Stroke and distance–Under penalty conditions when the player must return to the spot from which the ball was previously played and play another shot, while adding a penalty stroke, in effect, losing a stroke and the distance gained with the previous stroke.

Stroke play–A form of competition where the winner is determined by the player who takes the least number of total strokes. (See also **medal play**.)

Tee–The wooden or plastic implement on which the ball is placed for hitting the first, or "tee" shot on each hole. Also, the area designated as the starting place for each hole.

Tee box–The area designated as the starting place for each hole. (See also **tee**.)

Tee markers–Two markers placed on the teeing ground that mark the exact area where play should begin on each hole.

Teeing ground–The area designated as the starting place for each hole. (See also **tee**.)

Through the green–The entire golf course with the exception of the teeing grounds, putting greens, and hazards.

Topped shot–A rolling or bouncing shot that is caused when the ball is contacted above its equator low on the clubface or with the leading edge of the clubface.

USGA–United States Golf Association.

Up–The number of holes or strokes that a player is ahead of his opponent, e.g., two-up, three-up, etc.

Up and down–Holing out in two strokes from off the green.

Upright swing–A swing that is more vertical than normal. At the top of the backswing, the club is above the swing plane that was established at address.

Waggle–Movement of the club and/or the golfer, prior to starting the swing.

Whiff–To swing at the ball and completely miss it.

Winter rules–A local rule that allows golfers to move the ball to improve its lie. These are sometimes referred to as "preferred lies."

References

Ballard, Jimmy. *How to Perfect Your Golf Swing*. Trumbull, CT: Golf Digest/Tennis, 1981.

Boomer, Percy. *On Learning Golf*. London: Knopf, 1946

Bunker, L. and Owens, D. *Golf: Better Practice for Better Play*. Champaign, IL: Leisure, 1984.

Cochran, A. and Stobbs, J. *Search for the Perfect Swing*. Chicago: Triumph Books, 1996.

Coop, Richard. *Mind Over Golf*. New York: Macmillan, 1993.

Flick, Jim. *Jim Flick On Golf*. New York: Random House, 1997.

Flick, J. and Waggoner, G. *On Golf: Lessons from America's Master Teacher*. New York: Villard, 1997.

Gwyn, R. and Patch, C. How About A Long Putter? *Strategies*. 6(1), 15, 1992.

Gwyn, R. and Patch, C. Comparing Two Putting Styles For Putting Accuracy. *Perceptual and Motor Skills*. 76, 387–390, 1993.

Hebron, Michael. *See and Feel the Inside Move the Outside*. Smithtown, NY: Rost, 1984.

Henderson, I. and Stirk, D. *The Complete Golfer*. London: Victor Gollancz, 1985.

Hogan, Chuck. *Learning Golf*. Clifton, CO: Zediker, 1993.

Knudson, George. *The Natural Golf Swing*. Bellevue, WA: Kirsh & Baum, 1994.

Leadbetter, David. *The Golf Swing*. New York: Penguin, 1990.

Leadbetter, David. *Faults and Fixes*. New York: HarperCollins, 1993.

Leadbetter, David. *Positive Practice*. New York: HarperCollins, 1997.

McLean, Jim. "What Percentage of Golf Is Putting?," *PGA Magazine*, Volume 77, Number 4. Troy, MI: April, 1996.

McLean, J. and Dennis, L. *Golf Digest's Book of Drills*. Trumbull, CT: NYT Special Services, Inc., 1990.

Morrice, P. *The Golf Magazine Short Game Handbook*. New York: Lyons Press, 1999.

National Golf Foundation & LPGA. *Effective Strategies for Teaching and Coaching Golf*. 1994.

Pelz, Dave. *Dave Pelz's Short Game Bible*. New York: Broadway Books, 1999.

Pelz, D. and Frank, J. *Golf Magazine.* "Your Best Way to Putt." 45, 78–87, April, 2003.

Penick, Harvey. *Harvey Penick's Little Red Book.* New York: Simon and Schuster, 1992.

Penick, Harvey. *For All Who Love the Game.* New York: Simon and Schuster, 1995.

Penn State Sports Medicine Newsletter. "Visualization Techniques." Volume 2, Number 8. University Park, PA: April, 1994.

Peper, G., Frank, J. and Anderson, L. *Golf Magazine's Complete Book of Golf Instruction.* New York: Abrams, 1999.

Peper, George. *The Story of Golf.* New York: Cramer Productions, 1999.

PGA of America. *PGA Teaching Manual.* Palm Beach Gardens: PGA, 1990.

Rotella, Bob. *Golf Is a Game of Confidence.* New York: Simon & Schuster, 1996.

Straub, W.F. *Sport Psychology Analysis of Athlete Behavior.* Ithaca, NY: Mouvement, 1980.

Toski, B., Flick, J., and Dennis, L. *How to Become a Complete Golfer* (Rev. Ed.). Norwalk, CT: Golf Digest/Tennis, 1984.

United States Golf Association. *Rules of Golf.* Far Hills, NJ: USGA, 2002–2003.

Wiren, Gary. *Golf, Building a Solid Game* (2nd Ed.). Englewood Cliffs, NJ: Prentice Hall, 1992.

Wiren, Gary. *The Golf Magazine Course Management Handbook.* New York: Lyons, 1999.

Index